THE BRITISH ROYALTY COLLECTION

Profiles in History

LIAM DALE

The History Journals

Copyright © 2022 The History Journals | Liam Dale

No part of this book may be reproduced in any form or by any electronic or mechanical means, including information storage and retrieval systems, without written permission from the author or his representative, except for the use of brief quotations in a book review or media piece.

All pictures contained in this book are courtesy of www.thefootagelibrary.com

CONTENTS

Title Page
Copyright
KINGS & QUEENS of GREAT BRITAIN   1
BOUDICCA - THE WARRIOR QUEEN   21
ARTHUR: KING AND COUNTRY   51
RICHARD 1st – THE LIONHEART   71
MARY QUEEN OF SCOTS   100
Royal Romances - The British Monarchy   121
Royal Scandals & Conspiracies   142
PRINCESS DIANA   164
Royal Heritage   187
Would you please consider leaving a review?   209
FURTHER JOURNALS & BOOKS BY LIAM DALE INCLUDE   210
ABOUT THE AUTHOR   212

KINGS & QUEENS OF GREAT BRITAIN

60AD-2022

Anybody who visits London at the height of the summer will soon realize that the United Kingdom's capital city attracts sightseers from every far-flung corner of the globe. And what's on their list of attractions to see? Nine times out of ten it will be Buckingham Palace, often followed by the Tower of London, and since the tragic death of Diana, Princess of Wales in 1997, her former residence, Kensington Palace.

In an age when the monarchy, British or otherwise, is accused of being an outdated institution, the tourists still flock in their millions to follow in the footsteps of Royalty, both ancient and modern, to see for themselves the places where history was made.

When it comes to listing the great Kings and Queens of the past, there are undoubtedly some that are better remembered than others. Richard the Lion Heart, Henry the Eighth and King George the third are renowned for very different reasons and when it comes to the ladies, Mary the first, both, one of England and one of Scotland, Elizabeth the first and Queen Victoria are as fascinating today as when they were alive.

But there are many more characters worthy of investigation that are far less well known. So, whether you want a basic who's, who of the British Monarchy to help you in the next pub quiz, or you'd like to find out how we got from feuding tribes of Ancient Britons to the present day, prepare for a right Royal romp through the history books so that you never need to get your Henrys, Georges, Edwards, Richards, Marys and Williams mixed up again.

Before we get down to the nitty gritty of succession, it's well worth stepping back further in time to take a closer look at the British Isles just after the birth of Christ, when the Romans were masters of all they surveyed, including a large part of the United Kingdom. Of the native Brits, many of whom were Celts, there was considerable opposition to the Roman occupation, not least from the woman often dubbed the Queen of the Ancient Britons, Boudicca, or if you happen to be of a certain age, Boadicia.

This fearsome warrior Queen led her Iceni tribe to revolt against the Romans, and as neighboring tribes of Ancient Britons swelled their numbers, Boudicca led a campaign that advanced from Colchester all the way to London and beyond, until the Romans finally managed to stop her in her tracks.

Without actual records it is hard to be precise about dates, it's believed Boudicca came to prominence in about AD 61, but even after her death the Romans continued to have problems with the Celts. Rather than face the Scots in the North, who were as fearsome as the great warrior Queen, in AD 122, the Roman Emperor Hadrian built a wall to keep the Scots out of England. This early separation of the neighboring nations would continue for centuries, but more on that subject later!

Eventually the Roman Occupation came to an end when the overstretched Empire recalled their soldiers back to Rome but waiting in the wings were the bloodthirsty Saxons ready with invasion plans of their own. However, if legend is to be believed one man united the tribes of the British Isles to resist the Saxon advances, and it is quite possible that he came from Wales. We have all heard of King Arthur and his Knights of the Round Table, fighting for chivalry and honor in a lawless age, but try and find him in an historic timeline, and you really will struggle. A true Celt, Arthur is thought to have lived in the 5th Century AD, and this immediately gives us a major problem, historically.

Our images of King Arthur and his gallant Knights belong to a much later age, but there is a very good reason for this.

Way back in the 12th Century, a bishop known as Geoffrey of Monmouth wrote a "History of the Kings of Britain" and where the facts were a little sketchy, he simply filled in the blanks. Consequently, Geoffrey's rendition of the King Arthur story was set in the time that he knew best, his England was once more under threat of invasion, this time by the Danes, and this is how the story of the burnt cakes came about. Alfred escaped an attack by the Danes in the West Country and legend has it that he sought refuge with peasants living on the Somerset levels, while he contemplated how to save his Kingdom. One day when the peasant's wife went out on errands, Alfred was left in charge of her baking, but he was so caught up with matters of state, he forgot all about the cooking and was duly chastised when the woman returned to burnt cakes.

Whether true or not, this is the story that has gone down in the history books, when Alfred was in fact, as his name suggests, a much greater King than this footnote gives him credit for. After Alfred and a succession of Ed's of all varieties, including an Elder, a Fair and a Martyr, the next King that most of us will have heard of is Ethelred the Unready, who came to the throne in 978. However, it is a case of a meaning being lost in translation, because "Unraed", by which name he was actually called, means "poorly counselled" in Anglo-Saxon, and the unfortunate Ethelred might have benefited from some good advice.

The Danes were still on the rampage and Ethelred was no match for the Viking leader Sweyn Forkbeard, who seized the English throne in 1013. But Forkbeard's reign was short lived, as he died about five weeks later, and despite his wonderful name referring to the way he wore his beard, it's his son Canute who is much better remembered, and all because of another much-loved Royal legend.

King Canute ruled England from 1016, after a brief reversion to Ethelred's son, and he was one of the best monarchs the country had ever known. Wise and fair, Canute modernized the laws of the land, although many believe he considered himself so important he attempted to command the seas and the turn of the tide. However, this could not be further from the truth. Tired of his courtier's flattery, when one insisted Canute could order the tide not to come in, Canute went down to the beach, set up his throne at the water's edge and of course got wet, proving that he had no power over the elements, while at the same time exposing the courtier as very foolish indeed!

When Canute died, he was succeeded firstly by his son Harold and then his other son, Harthacanute. When he died the throne passed again back to the Saxon line and another son of Ethelred the Unready, who was also the half-brother of Harthacanute, known as Edward the Confessor, a title which was bestowed upon him because of his great piety. Nevertheless, Edward failed to produce a son and heir, and this caused a real problem, especially as it seems he promised the English throne to both his brother-in-law, Harold Godwinson and his distant cousin, William, Duke of Normandy.

Edward the Confessor died in 1066, a year familiar to us all because of the Battle of Hastings. When Harold became King, Cousin William over in France was not content to give up his claim to the English throne. William was also a descendent of Alfred the Great, and when he set out to conquer England, there was no stopping him. Harold was killed in the Battle of Hastings, depicted in the Bayeux Tapestry as being shot by an arrow through the eye, and the event heralded the Norman period of English history, quite literally changing the face of the nation during William's well-documented Norman Conquests.

When William was crowned King at the newly constructed Westminster Abbey, on Christmas Day 1066, he was ready to take control of the nation. Anglo-Saxon estates were confiscated and granted to Norman nobles, and the natives got very restless. William and his nobles put down many revolts, building their characteristic castles and fortresses all over the land, including the original White Tower of the Tower of London, constructed in 1078.

And to ensure his supremacy, William is also remembered for the compilation of the Domesday Book in 1085, an early form of census that recorded how land was being used, and more importantly for the Norman Treasury, how much tax could be levied on the people of England. Not that William lived long enough to personally reap the benefits as he died in 1087 after falling from his horse in France. It is important to remember that these early Kings were military leaders as well as monarchs and with lands in France and England, William certainly had his work cut out.

After William I came his son, William II, known as William Rufus because of his ruddy complexion. He too was kept busy, especially as the Scottish King Malcolm III tried, on more than one occasion, to invade his English neighbor, as did Welsh rebels unhappy with the Norman nobles occupying the boarder castles of the Marches. William Rufus however was not killed in battle, but in a hunting accident while out with friends in the New Forest, although the conspiracy theorists have a different version of events. Henry I, William's youngest brother was crowned at Westminster Abbey in 1100 and it has been suggested that he may have had a hand in his brother's untimely death.

Henry nonetheless pledged good governance and wisely neutralized any threat from Scotland by marrying the daughter of the troublesome, by now deceased, Malcolm III. But not everything ran to plan; his brother, the Duke of Normandy attempted to overthrow Henry, and the King lost his only son, William, who was drowned at sea. Now, this is where it gets interesting.

Henry 1 had a daughter, Matilda, who as a female was not expected to inherit the throne, but the King persuaded the Barons to accept her as his lawful successor. This may have been fine in theory, but when Henry died in 1135, Matilda was usurped by her cousin Stephen. Matilda may not have been crowned Queen, but she did not give up her claim to her father's throne without a fight. These were turbulent years characterized by Civil War, only brought to a satisfactory conclusion when Stephen agreed to name Matilda's son, Henry Plantagenet, Count of Anjou, as his heir.

Consequently, when Stephen died in 1154, he was the last Norman King of England, as Henry II became the first of the Plantagenets. It's obvious the Normans came from Normandy, but if you're wondering where the Plantagenets came from, it's all down to nickname. Geoffrey, Count of Anjou, Henry's father always wore a sprig of flowering Broom, Planta Genista and this is how he was known. When Henry II was crowned King of England in 1154, aged 21, he was already Count of Anjou and Toraine, as well as being Duke of Normandy and Aquitaine, which meant his French territories were more extensive than those owned by the King of France.

Add to that the throne of England, and Henry's Angevin Empire stretched from the Solway Firth to the Pyrenees. So far, we have focused on the monarchs, and not mentioned their Queens, but in the case of Henry II, his wife, Eleanor of Acquitaine has to be one of the most fascinating historical characters of all time. The pair were married in France in 1152, the bride being eleven years her handsome groom's senior. Eleanor had first been married to the King of France but had been granted an annulment because they were so closely related and when Henry came to the English throne, he brought with him a charismatic Queen, who was centuries ahead of her time.

Just as Alfred's remembered for burning the cakes, there is one incident that is synonymous with Henry II: the bloody murder of Thomas a Becket in Canterbury Cathedral in 1170. As monarch, Henry had been determined to control the power of the church and appointed his friend Becket to the influential post of Archbishop of Canterbury in 1162. But Becket would not be swayed from his religious principles and for eight years thwarted the King's reforms, enraging Henry so much, that on one occasion he screamed out "Will not someone rid me of this turbulent Priest".

Immediately four of Henry's Knights took him at his word and set off for Canterbury, and murdered Becket at the High Alter of the Cathedral. Whether this was the King's intention, or a tragic error, Henry II has gone down in the history books with blood on his hands. Other notable achievements in Henry's reign included the establishment of trial by jury and the acquisition of the title Lord of all Ireland, to go with all the others, in 1171 after a successful invasion. However, Henry II did not die a happy man.

His constant arguments with his wife resulted in her being confined to the French Castle of Chinon for years, and not surprisingly she sided with her son Richard in battle against her husband. Neither was his relationship with his sons much better and he refused to name an heir, until his dying breath in 1189, when he bequeathed the Angevin Empire to his third son Richard.

And so, we come to one of the best-loved English Kings of all time, Richard the Lionheart, friend of Robin Hood, Crusader Knight and darling of literature. But just as some Kings have been misrepresented as poor monarchs, Richard benefited from an over inflated reputation. Of the ten years Richard ruled, he only spent seven months of that time in England, while he plundered the nation's coffers and increased taxation to pay for his Crusades in the Holy Land.

Interestingly it is Richard's younger brother John who generally gets the blame for this heavy taxation, especially in the legends of Robin Hood. Richard the Lionheart was only forty-one when he died in 1199, shot by an archer in France, while he was in search of buried treasure, and his tomb can be found in Fontevrault Abbey next to those of his father Henry and his mother Eleanor, in the heart of the French countryside.

Like Henry II, Richard named his heir as he was dying, and it was his brother John, who has gone down in history, perhaps unfairly, as being as bad a King as Richard was good. King John's best known for signing the Magna Carta at Runnymede in 1215 to appease the warring Barons, and this historic document was crucial in the establishment of English Common Law. When John died a year later the English throne passed to his son, crowned King Henry III in 1216, at the age of nine, under a regency.

However, when Henry took full control in 1227, he proved to be a most unpopular King, and the Barons quietened by Magna Carta, were soon on the rampage again. It fell to Henry's eldest son Prince Edward to put the rebellion down, which he did with great relish. When Henry III died in 1272 Edward was on Crusade in the Holy Land but returned to be crowned King in 1274. Edward I is often known by the name Longshanks because he was very tall, and he was also renowned for his savagery towards opponents.

The Welsh certainly suffered at his hands when Wales was incorporated into his domain, and he was the first to appoint his eldest son Prince of Wales in 1301, a tradition that continues to this day.

However, he is most famous for his barbaric treatment of the Scots. After deposing the Scottish King in 1296 he stole the Stone of Destiny from Scone Palace, a historic artefact used in the Scot's coronation ceremony, and took it to Westminster Abbey where it remained until its return to Edinburgh Castle in 1996. Nevertheless, when Edward I invaded Scotland, he did not quite have it all his own way, thanks to the efforts of a now famous Scotsman by the name of William Wallace, whose armies beat the English at Sterling Bridge in 1297.

Edward did defeat the Scots a year later at Falkirk, when Wallace was captured and taken to London, where he was executed, but when Robert the Bruce was crowned King of Scotland in 1306, the oppressed nation North of the border served notice that the English now had a fight on their hands.

Upon the death of Edward I, in 1307, ironically on his way North for another go at invading Scotland, his son Edward II, the first ever Prince of Wales, was crowned king. The new King did not have the stomach for fighting the Scots, and Robert the Bruce assured Scottish Independence in 1314 when he routed the English at the Battle of Bannockburn. Yet Edward II's most dangerous adversary proved to his wife Queen Isabella, who ran off with her lover, Roger Mortimer, and the pair seized power in the name of the King's eldest son, again called Edward. Edward II was imprisoned in Berkeley Castle, where he was brutally murdered in 1327 on the orders of Isabella and has gone down in history as one of the most unfortunate Kings of all time. When Edward III finally seized power from the regency of Roger Mortimer in 1330, his 50-year reign proved him to be an affable King, much loved by his people. However, when he died in 1377, Edward's most notable contribution to the history books was his declaration of himself as heir to the French throne, starting what would become the Hundred Years War.

Sadly though, his eldest son, Edward the Black Prince pre-deceased his father, but having produced a son of his own before his untimely demise, Richard II came to the throne at the age of 10. Many believe Richard to have been a weak King, not least because of the play written by William Shakespeare about him. However, he crossed swords with his cousin Henry Bolinbroke, who deposed Richard in 1399 to become Henry IV, the first King of the House of Lancaster, a branch of the Plantagenets. But his prize proved to be something of a poisoned chalice, with nothing but revolts and treasury shortages, and he died a rather disappointed man in 1413.

Succeeded by his son Henry the fifth, Henry the fourth would no doubt have been extremely proud of his heir. After reviving the 100 Years War with France, his armies were victorious at the Battle of Agincourt, again made famous by one of Shakespeare's plays. As a result, upon his death in 1422, his son Henry VI became King inheriting both the English and French thrones. Henry VI was a good man, but a weak King and during his reign the English were thrown out of France after a campaign led in the first instance by Joan of Arc. The Plantagenet House of York also went into battle with Henry in the War of the Roses, which broke out in 1455, resulting in the Duke of York, the future Edward IV, deposing Henry in 1461.

After much too-ing and fro-ing, Henry VI was restored to the throne, but only for a very short time as he was murdered in the Tower of London, very possibly by the Duke of Gloucester who is also suspected of murdering Henry's son, who by rights would have become King. Consequently, Edward IV was restored to the English throne in 1471, the first King of the House of York. Despite his interrupted reign, Edward proved to be an able King who brought peace and prosperity to England, however when he fell out with his brother George, the unfortunate sibling sibling was found murdered in the Tower of London, something that was proving to be a regular occurrence.

When Edward IV died in 1483, his young son Edward succeeded him, however the boy's uncle claimed the child illegitimate and seized the throne for himself. The King in question was Richard

III and when Edward V and his younger brother, who were living in the Tower of London at the time, disappeared, suspicion certainly fell upon the new King. Richard III does not have the best of PR in Royal history, and Shakespeare certainly did little to improve matters with his play, which portrays the King as a hunchback. However, his two years on the throne are to this day a source of much fascination, but when he died at the Battle of Bosworth Field in 1485, defeated by one Henry Tudor, the War of the Roses were at an end, as a new age was about to begin.

Henry VII, with his Lancastrian ancestry married Elizabeth of York in 1486, uniting the two branches of the Plantagenet family as Tudors, but when his eldest son Arthur died in 1503, leaving his young widow, Catherine of Aragon, in the care of Henry the seventh, a remarkable chapter in history was about to be written. Henry VII died in 1509, and his second son, Henry VIII succeeded him. After receiving a dispensation from the Pope, the new King married Catherine of Aragon, his brother's widow, in the same year, in accordance with his father's wishes.

These were early days for the new Tudor dynasty and Henry was aware that he needed to produce an undisputed son and heir, an issue that would dominate his whole life, and create a religious rift throughout the nation that would cost many their lives.

Dutifully Queen Catherine produced child after child, including two boys who died in infancy, however the only surviving child was Mary, born in 1516. As Catherine, who was older than her husband, appeared less and less likely to produce an heir, Henry applied to the Pope for an annulment, claiming that his marriage was cursed because Catherine had been his brother's widow. When the Pope refused, Henry had the Act of Supremacy passed in 1533 making himself head of the English Church, breaking from Rome and Catholicism, so a divorce could be granted.

Henry went on to marry a further five times and as the rhyme goes, his wives were, Divorced, Beheaded, Died, Divorced, Beheaded, Survived, and here's a whistle stop tour of who's who. Henry married Anne Boleyn in 1533, but her only surviving child was a daughter, Elizabeth, and Anne was beheaded for adultery in 1536. Next Henry married Jane Seymour in 1536, eleven days after Anne's execution, and in 1537 she gave birth to Edward, the male child Henry had been waiting for.

But Jane's triumph was temporary, she died within weeks from postnatal complications. Henry next married Anne of Cleves on the strength of a portrait, but when he met her, she did not fulfil his expectations, and although he couldn't stop the wedding in 1540, the marriage was annulled six months later, as Henry claimed it had not been consummated.

Shortly after Anne of Cleves, Henry married the young, vivacious Katherine Howard in 1540, but like Anne Boleyn, she was accused of adultery and beheaded. The last of Henry's wives, Catherine Parr, who he married in 1543 managed to avoid the fates of her predecessors until the King's death in 1547, only to die in childbirth a year later, after marrying the brother of Henry's third wife, Jane Seymour. Although as Henry wished, his son Edward VI succeeded him, he was just a child of nine and the nation was governed by two Protectors.

However, when Edward contracted Tuberculosis, his days were numbered and he died in 1553 at the age of fifteen, leaving England, quite literally, in turmoil. The Duke of Northumberland, the then Protector of England when Edward fell sick, persuaded the boy to name Lady Jane Grey as his heir, in order to keep the nation protestant. Needless to say, Henry the eighth's daughter, Mary, believed she had a much greater claim to the throne, but was a devout Catholic, just as her mother, Catherine of Aragon, had been.

A pawn in a very dangerous game, the sixteen-year-old Lady Jane was manipulated onto the throne of England, as what history often calls the "Nine Days' Queen", but when Mary and her Catholic supporters arrived in London, the unfortunate Lady Jane was imprisoned in the Tower of London until her execution in 1554.

As soon as Queen Mary I took the throne, she set about restoring England to the Catholic faith, which she finalized in 1554, the same year that she married Philip of Spain. Many protestants who refused to convert to Catholicism were burnt as heretics, and therefore this Queen has gone down in history as "Bloody" Mary. Nevertheless, Mary suffered with the same anxiety as her father over producing an heir, and she failed to give birth to a live child.

To make matters worse her half-sister, Princess Elizabeth had many supporters keen to depose Mary in her favor, which would mean a return to a Protestant England, something the Queen could not countenance, and Elizabeth did well to come out of the Tower of London, where she was imprisoned at one stage, alive. When Mary died in 1558, at the age of 42, abandoned by Philip of Spain, and childless, the crown passed to Elizabeth, and the Church of England was quickly restored in 1559.

Throughout her reign, Elizabeth had many suitors, but she chose not to marry, claiming she was married to England. The Virgin Queen, as she became known, fought off the Spanish Armada, but the Catholics were a constant threat, and Elizabeth's cousin Mary, the Catholic Queen of Scotland, was used as a pawn in the fight for religious supremacy, just as Lady Jane Grey had been.

There's often confusion about Mary I of England and Mary I of Scotland, but for Elizabeth, Mary Queen of Scots, her cousin, was one of her biggest problems. Eventually faced with endless conspiracies with Mary seemingly at the heart of them, Elizabeth, who had kept Mary moving from castle to castle as her prisoner, finally signed her death warrant and had her executed in 1587.

Elizabeth I reigned for an incredible 45 years, but when she died in 1603 the inevitable problem of who would succeed the Virgin Queen meant the end of the Tudors. Ironically, it was the son of her cousin Mary Queen of Scots, James VI of Scotland, a Stuart, who became James I of England, at last uniting the nations to be governed by the same sovereign.

The people had loved Elizabeth, but James I was not a popular King and on the 5th of November 1605 Guy Fawkes and his fellow conspirators attempted to blow up the Houses of Parliament, and the King!

When James I died in 1625 his son Charles I, succeeded him, and was, like his father before him, a great believer in the Divine Right of Kings. Charles thought he was only answerable to God, and no one else, but eventually this resulted in Civil War, with the Parliamentarians, led by Oliver Cromwell in 1642.

When Charles and his Royalists were defeated, the King was tried and executed, leaving Britain without a monarchy for the Period of Interregnum, between 1649 and 1660, when the nation was overseen by the Lord protector, Oliver Cromwell. But Cromwell, just like the Kings in whose footsteps he had followed, planned for his son to succeed him.

However, Richard Cromwell simply was not up to the task, and in 1660 the monarchy was restored when the son of Charles I, yes, you've guessed it, Charles II, returned to carry on the Stuart line. Charles II was glamorous and brought an element of fun back to life after Oliver Cromwell's Puritanism, but he converted to Catholicism on his deathbed in 1685, and with no issue, the throne passed to his brother James II, a practicing Catholic who intended to restore links with Rome, even if it meant going to war.

However, when his wife gave birth to a son, a Catholic heir to the throne, tensions escalated. With a national crisis again developing over religion, the Protestant William of Orange was invited to take the English throne, to jointly rule with his wife Mary, the daughter of James II. The Royal Couple were crowned in 1689, after James II went to live in exile in France. Sadly, William and Mary had no children to follow them and after Mary's death from Smallpox in 1694 at Kensington Palace, William ruled on alone until his own death in 1702.

But the year before "The Act of Settlement" was passed to ensure a protestant succession, and when Queen Anne, the second daughter of James II came to the throne in 1702, by which time all her eighteen children had pre-deceased her, the nearest protestant relation was the German, Sophia, Electress of Hanover, who became her heir. Despite all the efforts made for a smooth protestant succession, Sophia died shortly before Queen Anne in 1714, so her son, George, who spoke no English, came to London to be crowned the first Hanoverian King.

This was far from popular with the British people and with a Jacobite rising starting in Scotland in 1715, planning to restore the Old Pretender, the Catholic son of James II, to the throne, all was not quite as straightforward with the Hanoverian succession as had been hoped. When George I died in 1727, he was succeeded by his son, George II, even though as Prince of Wales he had fought constantly with his father.

And history repeated itself as the new King's quarrels with his own son, Frederick, Prince of Wales, were legendary. And as well as disharmony on the domestic front, George II was still far from popular with the people of Britain. When the Jacobite's made another attempt to restore the Stuart line by putting Charles Edward Stuart, the Bonnie Prince, son of the Old Pretender, on the throne, they came incredibly close to succeeding. Bonnie Prince Charlie landed in Scotland in 1745 and after a conclusive victory over the British army at the Battle of Prestonpans, he marched south, and got as far as Derby, with London in his sights.

But a moment of indecision resulted in a retreat, with disastrous consequences, and the rebellion ended at the bloody battle of Culloden where the victorious British took their revenge. The Bonnie Prince fled to Skye, rowed by the lovely Flora MacDonald, before escaping to France, and the Hanoverian George II continued his reign. It is possible George II wasn't too troubled when his heir, Fredrick, the Prince of Wales, who he loathed, died unexpectedly after allegedly being hit on the head by a cricket ball, especially as he'd already ensured the succession having given the old King a grandson.

George II died in 1760, and his grandson became the next George in line, the third, and he was the first Hanoverian King born in Britain. Many believe George III was mad, and he certainly showed all the signs of being so, on several occasions. What he suffered from was a physical condition called Porphyria that gave every indication of mental illness. But like all the Georges who had preceded him, George III had a poor relationship with his eldest son the Prince of Wales, who he considered a disgrace because of his wild living.

Nevertheless, the future George IV had to take over as Regent because of his father's ill health between 1811 and the King's death in 1820. When finally crowned as George IV, the Prince who had waited so long to be King had a relatively short reign of just over ten years and one of his main claims to fame is the fact that he transformed Buckingham House into the beautiful Royal palace we know and love today.

And finally, after George IV, Britain got a King with a different name, William IV, his predecessor's brother. Despite speculation about fathering numerous offspring, George IV had only one legitimate daughter, who died in 1817, leaving no issue. William IV was 64 when he became King and despite having plenty of illegitimate offspring, he had no issue to legally succeed him.

When he died in 1837 it was the end of the line for the Hanoverian men, and the crown passed to an 18-year-old niece of William IV, by the name of Victoria.

For historians, the reign of Queen Victoria is a great source of fascination, as she managed to restore the popularity of the monarchy in Great Britain. When Victoria married the German Prince Albert, to honor him, the Royal House became known as Saxe-Coburg-Gotha, and their happy union produced nine children who would marry into all the major European Royal Families.

It is hard to find much Queen Victoria had in common with her Hanoverian predecessors except that both she and Albert found the wild behavior of their eldest son, the Prince of Wales, intolerable, resulting in a very strained relationship.

When Prince Albert died in 1861 the Queen was distraught and blamed the behavior of the Prince of Wales for her husband's death. Waiting to become Edward VII was going to go on for many years and when Queen Victoria died in 1901, after more than 50 years on the throne, the new King was destined for much shorter reign.

As the 20th Century dawned, Edward VII brought with him a sense of freedom to the people of Britain after the constraints of the Victorian age, but when he died in 1910, the threat of war with Germany was looming large. George V had never imagined he would become King as the second son of Edward VII, but when his older brother died unexpectedly, he took his responsibilities very seriously, and was a popular King at a time when his German ancestry could have been a problem.

The German Kaiser, William II, causing all the problems, was a cousin of the British King, who considerately changed the name of the Royal House from the German Saxe-Coburg-Gotha to Windsor, showing precisely where his loyalties lay. Nevertheless, World War I, fought between 1914 and 1918 resulted in the King suffering ill health in the post war years, and when he died at Sandringham in 1936, another War with Germany was threatening to disturb the peace.

At such a difficult time politically, everyone had high hopes of the new King, Edward VIII, the eldest son of George V, but his love for the American divorcee, Wallis Simpson resulted in his abdication in December 1936. The responsibility for saving the British monarchy on this occasion fell to the quietly spoken Duke of York and his young family, and with little time for preparation he became King George VI, as Britain again headed for War. George VI had two daughters, and the eldest Elizabeth, became the Heiress Presumptive, with more time than her father to get used to the idea of becoming Queen.

Again, like his father before him, George VI found himself King of a nation at war in 1939, and the seven years of the Second World War took a considerable toll on his health. Yet the young Princess Elizabeth could never have guessed she would lose her father and become Queen quite as soon as she did. When George VI died in 1952 the new Queen Elizabeth II promised herself to the nation, and her coronation in Westminster Abbey in 1953 was watched by people everywhere, as it was televised.

Moving into the media age Queen Elizabeth II has seen her family face a hungry world press, constantly searching for the latest Royal news stories. In 1981 her eldest son, Charles, the Prince of Wales, married Lady Diana Spencer, and their every move was under scrutiny. After securing the succession with two sons, Princes William and Harry, the marriage sadly ended in divorce in 1996, and a year later Diana, princess of Wales was killed in a tragic car accident on the streets of Paris.

As a result, the Queen has carried the responsibility for leading her family well into the 21st Century, as she still works tirelessly to guide the future heirs to the throne as they too face a lifetime of service to the nation.

And on that very positive note, as the next generation of the British monarchy steps "into the breach" as William Shakespeare so eloquently put it, who can say what the future might bring. We have all come a long way from Boudicca, the Queen of the Ancient Britons, leaving a wake of destruction wherever she went, to Elizabeth II leading gently but firmly by example, leaving mostly only happy memories for those of her adoring people, fortunate enough to meet her. As the history books tell, even with Royalty, things do not always necessarily go to plan, with happy ever after endings, but one thing is absolutely for certain: A monarchy that can adapt to the age in which they live will always survive and get stronger, whatever might have gone before.

LIAM DALE

◆ ◆ ◆

BOUDICCA - THE WARRIOR QUEEN

60-61AD

When it comes to women in history, there are few that command the respect that Boudicca, the warrior Queen of the Ancient Britons, has achieved over the centuries, yet this fearsome female remains to this day a true enigma. Who she was, what she did, and the consequences of her actions are as fascinating as they have ever been and this journal will take you on a journey of discovery to find the real Boudicca, the woman beyond the legend.

Nearly 2,000 years ago, this widowed Queen, was one of the few souls brave enough to rise in rebellion against the mighty Romans who were occupying her homeland. She managed to amass and control an army of over one thousand Ancient Britons, laying waste to several of the nation's occupied towns and cities along the way, including London, before eventually succumbing to the dominance of the Roman Empire in one final, huge battle in 61 A.D.

This is the history of Boudicca in a nutshell, but before we go any further, we have an important issue to straighten out. It was William Shakespeare who famously posed the question "What's in a name?" in his play "Romeo and Juliet", but it could equally have been asked of the heroine of our story.

Here's a quick puzzle. Pick the odd one out...
Boudicca, Boadicea, Buduica, Bonduca, or Mrs Prasutagus?

You may have thought the odd one out was Mrs Prasutagus, as the rest of the variations seem to be different ways of saying (and spelling) the name of this incredible woman. However, Mrs Prasutagus is the one option that goes without query, as she was without doubt the wife of Prasutagus, the King of the Iceni Tribe, Iceni/Icineye, being yet another major area for debate on pronunciation.

So, the answer to the question is that there is no odd one out, each variation has been used at some stage throughout history, but for this journal we'll stick with Boudicca, which seems to be the modern accepted form of this great lady's name.

Boudicca would have been derived from the Celtic word Bouda which means victory. Today we tend to associate the term Celtic with the people of Ireland, Scotland and Wales, but this collection of noble and warlike people, from the late 5th Century BC onwards, populated many other countries, including Austria, Switzerland, Norway, Germany, France, Denmark, Belgium, Spain, Italy, Greece, Finland, Portugal and of course England, Boudicca's homeland.

The name Celt derives from the Latin, *Celtae*, Latin being the language spoken throughout the Roman Empire, which included many of the countries where the Celts resided. But more of the Celts and their colorful traditions a little later.

So, if Boudicca was named after the Celtic Goddess worshipped by the Iceni tribe, then this may not have been the Queen's real name at all, but just the name given to her by her followers as she led them into battle.

The Iceni tribe, who Boudicca became leader of after her husband Prasutagus's death, occupied most of the English region known as East Anglia and to be more specific the counties of Norfolk and Suffolk, with the town of Thetford being at the heart of Boudicca's domain. We know this because of the writings of the Roman historian, Tacitus, who took an interest in the courageous and battle-hardy Queen of Ancient Britons. It's said that history is only told by the victors, and this is never more evident than in the case of Boudicca. Her story has only been passed down through the centuries as a result of the Roman accounts of her, but only after she had been defeated.

Interestingly Tacitus took a great interest in Britain, because his father-in-law had served there as a military tribune under Suetonius Paulinus during the time of Boudicca's uprising, and it's highly likely that he was able to give Tacitus an eyewitness account of the events. But, with archaeological research and reading between the lines of Roman boasting and bravado, it is possible to form our own picture of this mighty rebellious woman.

Time then to expand on the legend of Boudicca, who is still regarded as one of Britain's greatest leaders, alongside the giant men of British history, including King Arthur, Winston Churchill, Robin Hood, and King Richard the `Lionheart. After all, who says all legendary heroes must be men?!

It all began with Britain being invaded by the Romans. But, before we get into the swords, the fighting, the shields, the helmets, the flags, the war cries, the chariots, the spears, the togas, the laurel wreaths, the guts and gore, let's pause a moment and travel back through time a little further than Boudicca, to experience a flavour of the Roman Empire itself.

Around 700 years before the birth of Jesus Christ, the city of Rome was built. At first, it was ruled by Kings and then, when the last King, Tarquin the Proud, was overthrown because of his barbaric cruelty to his people, Rome became a Republic. This is essentially a country with a King, Queen or an Emperor, but with an elected ruling body. Rome's Republic was ruled by a Senate, made up of elected Senators, very much like the United

States of America, all with different responsibilities.

With a powerful military tradition as the advancing Roman Army became more powerful, the city of Rome itself became the capital for an ever-expanding Roman Empire. The Romans dominated wherever they advanced, from France to North Africa, and they eventually appointed an Emperor to rule over all their territories. This was since the Generals who controlled the various legions of the Roman Army couldn't agree on a single decision, which made controlling the Roman Empire a task fraught with constant bickering and backstabbing. Of course, this isn't to say that this all stopped when an Emperor was appointed, in fact, in some cases it got worse.

Even with a troop of special soldiers to protect him, called the Praetorian Guard, many of the more unpopular Emperors were often attacked or even assassinated, sometimes by the very soldiers who were supposed to be protecting them.

Whereas, in Britain the Celts dominated, but they were far from being a big happy family either. Made up of tribes, often ruled by Kings, Queens, or Chiefs, they usually lived in settlements where a large hill could be used as a vantage point to defend themselves from attackers. Often, a fortification would be built on a hill, like a very early form of a Castle, as can still be seen across East Anglia. In fact, one of the lowest Hillforts, just 6 feet above sea level, can be found at Stonea Camp, near the town of March, in Cambridgeshire.

Amidst the Norfolk fens, this region is a popular walking area that covers three counties in eastern England and used to be known as the 'wetlands' because of its soggy nature! This is believed to be the site where a huge battle took place between the Iceni tribe, 20 years before Boudicca was Queen, and an invasion force of the Roman Army, who were on a reconnaissance mission to see whether Britain would be a viable place to conquer and add to the empire.

Around the time of Boudicca, Stonea Camp would have been a very wet place, with the ditches filled with water. Archaeological excavations have uncovered horribly mutated adult and child skeletons at Stonea Camp, with indents of Roman swords cut right into the bones, proving that a battle did take place at Stonea, between the Iceni and the Roman Army.

Nevertheless, fighting off invaders was never the highest priority for the Celts, as they were often preoccupied with fighting amongst themselves. Neighboring tribes of Celts were never at ease with one another and were frequently engaged in arguing or fighting over something, very much like siblings in a large extended family.

The invasion of Britain by the Romans began in earnest during the year 55 B.C. Julius Caesar, probably the most famous of the Roman Emperors, conquered France, then known as Gaul, in this year before turning his attention across the Channel to England.

In fact, Julius Caesar tried to conquer Britain twice, once in 55 B.C. and then two years later in 54 B.C. and both attempts failed. This was due to the ferocity of the British warriors, who never fought in massed ranks or with tactical precision like their Roman counterparts, battling to the death with anger, with passion, and with pride. One of the other major stumbling blocks for the Roman Army was the British weather. The rain, cold, wind, and the odd spot of sun, made invading a land with no roads virtually impossible.

Dirt tracks were about all that joined the tribes in each area together and there was little adequate shelter as the Ancient Briton's were a hardy people who lived in homes that were little more than mud huts, with roofs of straw, that barely kept out wind and the rain. This was a far cry from the type of living conditions the sophisticated Romans were used to. The British may continually bemoan the weather but, in this instance, it was actually a great help to the natives and not a hindrance at all.

A hundred years later, with the new Roman Emperor Claudius in charge, they decided to have another go at invading Britain. This time, with the knowledge acquired from the previous attempts, the Romans succeeded in their conquest.

The Romans made peace with some of the Celtic tribes, allowing them to still rule over their small territories, and 'client kingdoms' were born. 'Client kingdoms' enabled Rome to maintain control by appointing a King from within the tribe, who would be loyal to them. The Romans would take a third of the tribe's harvest away from them every year, home-grown food and hand-reared animals, and the tribe would then be forced to buy it back again at a higher price than they were paid for it in the first place. Not surprisingly this enraged some of the tribes, who continued to fight with the conquering army, instigating little pockets of resistance against the Romans, all over the country.

However, it wasn't until 61 A.D. that the Romans had to deal with that most dangerous threat of all; a woman scorned. As we already know, Boudicca was married to Prasutagus, who was the Roman-appointed leader of the Iceni tribe, which was all fine and good until he died. Being a wise sort of a fellow, well used to dealing with the Romans, he left a will that split all his land and possessions between his wife, Boudicca and the new Roman Emperor, Nero. The Romans did tend to get through rather a lot of Emperors, thanks to plotting and scheming, murder and mayhem, and some were better than others. Unfortunately, Nero was a disaster for Rome and proved to be equally bad news for Boudicca as well.

Nero wasn't satisfied with Rome's cut of Prasutagus's will, and not only demanded that Boudicca step down as Queen, but also that as well as taking most of their harvest every year, Rome would demand the payment of large taxes from the already-starving Iceni.

Understandably, this enraged Boudicca and her refusal to comply resulted in the Romans instigating a campaign to publicly humiliate her. On orders from Rome her tribe were forced to witness her being flogged with whips and beaten with wooden rods, and in turn Boudicca was made to watch her two young daughters violated by Roman soldiers. A Roman historian wrote of her, after witnessing this appalling public humiliation, that she stood defiant and unbowed.

> *"She was very tall, and her aspect was terrifying, for her eyes flashed fiercely and her voice was harsh. A mass of red hair fell down to her hips, and around her neck was a twisted gold necklace."*

In an unprecedented show of support, the neighbouring Celtic tribes rose in anger alongside Boudicca forming a viable resistance to such barbaric treatment and together the huge army marched from Thetford to the capital of Roman Britain, Colchester, and promptly destroyed it.

Boudicca's fearsome army then stormed through Essex, before targeting London, and then St Albans in Hertfordshire, to meet out some equally bloody revenge.

The Romans re-gathered their troops, as some of them were fighting to overthrow rebellious tribes of Welsh Celts, marching them back from the far-flung Island of Anglesey. The final battle between Boudicca's irrepressible Celts and the might of the Roman Empire is believed to have taken place in the village of Mancetter, near the town of Atherstone, in the county of Warwickshire, England. This was on the Roman Road called Watling Street, which stretched with Roman precision from Dover to Shropshire, and the ensuing battle went down in history as The Battle of Watling Street. Boudicca's Army was massacred, in part due to the battlefield discipline and superior military tactics of the Roman Army, but despite the rebellion being crushed her passionate stand against barbaric tyranny had given the Romans the shock of their lives!

But we'll return for a more detailed view of Boudicca's last stand a little later; first we'll take that promised closer look at the Celts.

The name Celt originated with the ancient Greeks, who called the barbarian people of Central Europe "Keltoi". The area where they lived became a constantly changing collection of tribal "nations". The Celts were never an "Empire" ruled by one government; instead, they are thought to have originated in central Europe (Southern Germany, Austria, and Hungary, for example). From around 3,500 years ago, the Celts began moving across the Continent, and eventually inhabited a large portion of Europe.

Weapons were very important to the Celts, and they would sacrifice their finest swords, shields, spears and even chariots to the gods by throwing them into lakes, rivers and bogs, places they considered to be sacred. On the island of Anglesey, in North Wales, an important location for later in the Boudicca story, archaeologists have found over 150 bronze and iron objects, including shields, daggers, swords, chariot fittings and harnesses in a marshy bog. The dredging and digging that took place has transformed the area into a lake, so it's unlikely that anything else will be discovered, but the collection reflects just how militaristic and proud the Celts were, and because of similar collections in the South of England, they undoubtedly also traded items as a major part of their culture.

For the Celts, religion was closely tied to the natural world and all that Mother Nature provided. They worshipped their Gods and Goddesses in so-called sacred places as mentioned earlier, like rivers and lakes, even taking themselves to the cliff tops to worship, with the beautifully significant White Cliffs of Dover being of equal importance to the Ancient Britons, as they are to us today.

The Celts were also convinced that the world of the supernatural governed every aspect of the world that they knew, with the most powerful being the sun, the moon and the stars, and many of their celebrations and rituals reflected this, with some having been passed down through the ages. Just look at Stonehenge, one of Britain's most treasured ancient monuments.

To this day we really have little idea of the purpose of these fine stones, but as traditional Druids gather here to celebrate the summer solstice each year, our best guess is that this positively Herculean construction was somehow connected with sun worship, so intrinsic to Celtic beliefs.

As a contrast, the everyday lives of the Celts were on a much simpler scale and there are places where even in the 21st Century we can go to find about how Queen Boudicca and her people lived.

Cinderbury Fort in Gloucestershire is a reconstruction of an Iron Age settlement, which truly demonstrates what Celtic life would have been like. The Celts were a proud, artistic race of people and this showed in every aspect of their lives. They wove their own cloth, were wonderful potters and incorporated highly decorative design into their metalworking. In fact, looking at Cinderbury amazing huts in detail, they are indeed a work of art. The wooden frame has been covered in clay to make hard walls, and thatch was often used to keep out the rain. An iron cauldron would have hung over a fire for cooking and creating warmth, while a domed clay oven would have provided the Celts with their daily bread.

The Celts were very practical people, but they were also very spiritual, worshiping as we heard earlier an entire range of Gods and Goddesses. They even had their own priests, called Druids, who led religious ceremonies and acted as judges and advisers within Celtic society. However, as a race they were undoubtedly best known for their fierceness on the battlefield. These people that quietly lived tending to their animals, making pots and metalworking in settlements, would fight to the death when they were under threat, believing that death was simply a journey to their "Otherworld".

Consequently, the Celts showed no fear whatsoever in battle, which even the disciplined Roman Army had no answer for. Who knows, this might just be another explanation of why so many swords and so much weaponry got thrown into lakes, or at least got buried with its deceased owners, to help them in the Otherworld. Incidentally a Celt believed that if you died in the Otherworld, which was possible, you would be born again on earth, to do all that fighting again!

While we're still about throwing swords into lakes, understanding the Celts can help to demystify another right royal Great British legend. Boudicca fought to be Queen of the Ancient Britons against the Romans, but when the Romans finally left Britain many years later, King Arthur was crowned the last Celtic Monarch. Legend has it that young Arthur drew a sword from a stone to prove his right to rule, but could this have been a mere distortion of history?

The Celts were great fans of single combat, where two tribal leaders would often fight on behalf of their people for supremacy. The Druids would oversee the proceedings, while the symbol of Kingship was not a crown, but instead a sword. The sword was placed on an altar, usually made of stone, and watched over by the Druids until it was bestowed upon the victor. Could it have been a sword ON a stone, rather than in it? Also, the legend of Arthur, claims that his sword was returned to the Lady of the Lake after his death, again immortalizing the Celtic practice of throwing swords into sacred bodies of water.

But that's of course another story altogether, so let's return to the more unusual Celtic practices that Boudicca would have known very well.

Celtic people had great respect and reverence, for of all things, the human head. This wasn't just by looking in mirrors and admiring the braiding in their hair or the tattoos over their faces. No. That would be too simple. The Celts, according to Roman historians, cut off the heads of their dearly departed family members and worshipped their skulls, by encircling them with candles and praying. The Celts were also renowned for cutting off the heads of their enemies too, so that they could remove the brain and mix it with lime to make it into a hard-round ball. They could then carry this into battle to give them the strength of their enemy as well as their own. Failing that, when they ran out of objects to throw, a well-hardened brain could make a very handy missile indeed!

Throughout Celtic history, the head of the tribe could just as easily be a King or a Queen. There were no stereotypical sexist views from the Celts, as they believed that women were equal to men, with Boudicca being the prime example of this. The title of King or Queen was not necessarily inherited, for monarchs could nominate their successor, however when the Romans invaded Britain, they appointed the head of the tribe to ensure the people's allegiance to Rome.

The Romans came to Britain looking for riches; land, slaves, and most of all, iron, lead, zinc, copper, silver and gold. The Romans took over the Celts' land and built their own towns, with strong forts linked by a good road system that is still in evidence today. Ports and harbours were also important places for the Romans to bring in food, wine and oil from abroad.

You can constantly find examples of the Roman occupation of Britain, ranging from the grandiose splendour of the baths in Bath, to remains of Roman Villas, like the ones tucked into the rural hillside of the Cotswolds. The major Roman settlements close by were at Glevum, modern day Gloucester and Corrinium, the lovely market town of Cirencester.

If you visit these sites today, looking across the valleys, the hills are beautiful, but for the Roman settlers there was danger lurking high above them. About a mile as the crow flies from the Glevum Roman remains, on a hilltop, you'll find another set of remains, this time from a once magnificent Iron Age Hill Fort with a vantage point from which the Celts could have seen any would-be attackers. In Boudicca's day, the hill would have been fortified with ditches and ramparts, and although you need a little imagination to visualise what it would have been like, at least having seen the reconstructed huts at Cinderbury you have a better idea.

However, even those who come here with a dedicated interest in Iron Age and Celtic archaeology, will be amazed by the magnificent panoramic view, and go away impressed at the Ancient Briton's ability to choose a beautiful place to live, even if they lacked the home comforts of the Romans in the valley below.

Having seen how closely the Romans and Celts lived together; it's understandable that relations were not always unfriendly.

The Roman way of life was very different from that of the Celts, and many started to copy the Romans, speaking their language and living like them. The Celts started using Latin words and within a few generations the Celtic and Roman ways of life became mixed, with marriages taking place between them; Roman soldiers retiring from the army to become farmers and artisans in Celtic tribes, and sons and grandsons of those who fought against the Romans even joining the Roman army.

In Wales, Scotland, Ireland, the Isle of Man, Cornwall and Brittany across the channel in France, the Celtic culture has survived and many of us including me still regard ourselves as Celts to this day.

With our greater understanding of the life that Boudicca and her people lived, and the traditions and beliefs that shaped the way that they behaved we'll now return to the story of this great warrior Queen and take a closer look at her incredible story.

The best place to start is by taking a journey to the area of Britain where the Iceni tribe lived, ruled over by King Prasutagus, and then taken over by Queen Boudica after his death. The tribe occupied lands situated in the counties of Norfolk and Suffolk. Unlike the Roman invaders, who had set up luxury towns and homes, the Iceni tribe as we've already read would've lived relatively simple lives. The palace that King Prasutagus and Queen Boudicca ruled their tribe from would've been made of entirely perishable materials, like wood, clay, straw, mud, and even animal dung, even if it had been on a grander scale than the charming huts at Cinderbury.

But Cinderbury is far from being the only place in the Britain where you can experience first-hand what the life of an Ancient Briton was like. If you visit the county of Norfolk, in southeastern England, you will find an actual reconstruction of a genuine Iceni tribe village, which is situated at the village of Cockley Cley, near the town of Swaffham. There are all sorts of treasures to discover including the dubious delights of a snake pit, hanging skeletons, stocks and a pillory, plus the usual Celtic roundhouses and forges for smelting iron and fashioning ornate weapons. This is about as close as we can ever get to an exact replica of the village that Queen Boudicca would've lived in and, although this isn't the real thing, there is evidence that the Cockley Cley site had a Celtic settlement based here when our heroine was waging such bloody war against the Romans.

The town of Thetford, the actual seat of power of Boudicca's Iceni tribe, is not far from Cockley Cley and is well worth a visit if you are in the area. There are remnants of the defensive works that would've protected the settlement from attack and the fascinating Castle Hill stands as a proud testament to this, for modern day tourists. Castle Hill is to the east of Thetford, and is a massive mound, probably about 80 feet in height, and 1000 feet in diameter, that dates to the time of Boudicca. Wherever you happen to be unearthing Celtic settlements across the country it's evident that wherever possible the Celts favored the high ground, which must have been a terrifying prospect for their enemies.

There's no denying that the Boudicca story, if it was a work of fiction, would top the historical best seller charts with immediate effect and even in the 21st Century few can fail to feel anything but empathy for this great woman, literally centuries before her time.

Having had a look around the Iceni tribe's home, and done our background research on the period in history when this all took place, what was Boudicca really like? She was the archetypal heroine, courageous, tempestuous, the well-respected Queen of the Iceni Tribe, with flame-red hair to match her fiery temperament. Also, she was far from being alone enjoying great status as a woman warrior, because the Celtic people were noted for allowing their wives and daughters to join in any battle with them.

Although historians claim that Celts were no more than illiterate barbarians, with a rudimentary knowledge of farming that helped to keep them alive between battles, inter-tribal-fighting and general skirmishes, they were wise enough to allow women to operate on an equal footing to men in all aspects of their culture. Boudicca's husband died whilst her daughters were still very young, and it's believed that she was in her late thirties at the time this happened.

And what of the love interest? Prasutagus was Boudicca's older husband, who had taken over as leader of the Iceni tribe when the Roman invasion reached Britain's shores. The Romans allowed the Iceni to keep their land so long as Prasutagus as King of the tribe did as they asked and kept paying the taxes. Needing a Queen, he married Boudicca, who was of the Celtic nobility, and they had two daughters.

Prasutagus had been clever enough to keep the Romans happy but he was also wise enough to know that if he died there would be difficulties so he left a will that he thought would resolve matters nicely. He bequeathed half of his money, his personal possessions and the Iceni lands, which consisted of Norfolk and Suffolk, governed from Thetford to Boudicca and his daughters. Because he had daughters rather than sons, he needed to ensure that they would have enough money for a dowry so that they could marry well.

Also, Boudicca needed to be able to govern as Queen of the Iceni and pay taxes to the Romans until she could marry again and hand over some of the responsibility. The other half his legacy was left to the Roman Emperor Nero, in the hope of appeasement. Unfortunately, the Emperor Nero was not one of Rome's most reasonable citizens and he greedily decided that he wanted everything Prasutagus left for himself.

Without doubt, returning to our historical novel scenario Nero would have to be classed as the true villain of the peace. This was one of Rome's most notorious Emperors, who became corrupted by absolute power, absolutely! His mother, Messalina, had married the Emperor Claudius, her own Uncle, as a means of gaining wealth and power. Through her scheming and conniving, she managed to get Claudius to adopt Nero as his own son, and thereby make him rightful heir to the Roman Empire.

But before the ink was even dry on the statute, Messalina poisoned Claudius, and, at the age of fourteen, Nero became the new Emperor of Rome. Spoiled beyond all measure, he loved living life to excess; he married frequently, divorced regularly and had many of his wives and a whole host of lovers, of both sexes, murdered, just because he'd got bored with them!

Nero also considered himself to be a great artist and performer, although it was considered shameful for a Roman emperor to appear as a public entertainer, acting, singing, and playing his lyre (a type of small harp). Never one to bow to public opinion he continued to do exactly as he pleased and never once left Rome as other Emperor's had done, to see the territories claimed for the Empire and congratulate the army on their conquests. When a great fire devastated Rome in July of 64 A.D., just a few years after the death of Boudicca, Nero was accused of starting it himself to make way for a new and more glorious palace that he wanted to build, made entirely of Gold.

So, when the Emperor Nero decided to steal the rest of the money, lands and possessions from the widowed Queen Boudicca, it wouldn't have come as a great surprise to anyone. Neither would it have been a shock that Boudicca and her daughters were treated so barbarically upon Nero's orders, and from the point of view of an epic saga their humiliation and violation at the hands of the Roman soldiers proved pivotal in rallying the Celts, who generally fought amongst themselves, to revolt against Rome. And if the story now calls for rage and retribution, this is exactly what the Romans were about to get.

With the neighboring Celtic client kingdoms fired up and ready to follow Boudicca as their leader, the Romans had to face their biggest threat on British soil to date. The southeast corner of England was predominantly made up of these small 'client kingdoms', as the Romans christened them, which were still ruled by the Celts but under strict Roman control. Nevertheless, there was always an uneasy sense that the status quo could be very easily upset.

In fact, although the Romans had successfully invaded Britain, they had never quite managed to truly conquer it. In the west, particularly in Wales, it took 30 years of continual battling before the Celts finally succumbed to Roman rule. The further

North the Romans advanced, the more difficult they found the terrain, the weather, and the people. Sixty years after Boudicca's humiliation in front of her own tribe, the Romans gave up trying to conquer Scotland, or Caledonia, as the Romans called it, building Hadrian's Wall to prevent military raids by the Scottish tribes of Celts into Roman occupied England.

This stone and turf fortification stretched across the breadth of Great Britain, of which a significant portion still exists, specifically in the middle section, and historians and preservation societies are unanimously agreed when they call it the most important monument built by the Romans in Britain.

Returning to our story though, the plot is set to reach its conclusion as Boudicca gathered up as many rebellious tribes as she could, convincing everyone to put aside their differences in order to go to war against their common enemy, the Romans.

From the town of Thetford, Boudicca and the massed Celtic Army of one hundred thousand soldiers marched straight for the Roman stronghold of Camulodunum, now known as Colchester, which was dominated by retired Roman officers and their families. At that time, the town of Colchester was the capital of Roman Britain, so it was the ideal place to attack first.

However, before the Roman's arrival it had been the main base of the Trinovantes tribe, who also claimed the county of Essex and part of Suffolk as their home, before their lands had been seized from them. Many of their people had been enslaved and they'd also been ordered to pay taxes to the Romans for their own land, just like the Iceni. Previously the Trinovantes had feuded constantly with Boudicca's Iceni tribe until the differences were put aside to revolt against the Romans. Colchester had many fine examples of Roman buildings and architecture, including council chambers, a theatre and the massive Roman Temple to Claudius, Nero's predecessor, the murdered uncle.

Boudicca's Army dramatically outnumbered the inhabitants of Colchester, as many of the soldiers that should've been stationed there were away fighting the Celts in Wales. Colchester today seems rather proud of Boudicca, even though she destroyed their town. She's even been commemorated in a stained-glass window in Colchester Town Hall.

Boudicca, by now a warrior Queen in every sense of the word, and her Celtic Army, completely devastated the town of Colchester, burning down the Roman Temple of Claudius, its opulence, grandeur and sophistication representing everything that the Celts hated about the Romans. A grand Castle was later built on the vaulted foundations of the Roman Temple of Claudius and today, this is the home of the Colchester Castle Museum, at the eastern end of the High Street.

If you visit the museum, you can experience an audio-visual drama all about Boudicca's reasons for burning the town to the ground. The museum also exhibits charred remains of fruit, grain, pottery, and bedding from the time, as well as the decapitated skulls of Roman soldiers.

Among the highlights on show are two Roman military tombstones. When they were discovered, they were broken in two and found face down in the ground. A local historian believes this happened at the time of the revolt and some recent finds at a London cemetery bear out his theories that the desecration of sacred burial grounds was a feature of Boudicca's rebellion.

Putting together the pieces that archaeologists have discovered most of the Roman residents of Colchester crammed into the vaults of the Temple, barricading themselves away from the invading Celts. But Boudicca remember, was a woman scorned and no mercy was shown, or quarter given, as they were all burned alive. However, compared to the violent deaths the marauding Celts inflicted on other Roman citizens of Colchester, it was perhaps a better option. Although there is no sign of the Roman Temple above ground, the vaults where so many Romans died are still to be found below the Castle, and if you're not afraid of ghosts you can take a guided tour around the vaults if you visit the Colchester Castle Museum.

And just for added interest, in the basement of an old Coaching Inn called 'The George', on the main High Street, not too far away from the Colchester Castle Museum, there is a pane of glass that protects a cutaway section of the soil that has been built upon over the years. It's about 6 feet below the surface and near the top you can see a distinctive layer of bright red burnt clay. This is all that remains of the wattle-and-daub buildings of the Celts that became, when burned, a hard, red clay, and this is often referred to as the 'Boudiccan Destruction Layer'.

But for now, we'll leave Colchester smouldering behind us, as another exciting male protagonist comes to join the story. With a final showdown between Boudicca and her Ancient Britain's and the Roman army already looming large, we meet the commander of the opposition. The Roman soldiers, fighting in Wales at the time of the burning of Colchester, were led by Gaius Suetonius Paulinus and as soon as the news broke of Boudicca's terrible attack, the Roman Army was mobilized, marching southeast in order to stop the Warrior Queen in her tracks.

Suetonius Paulinus was the Roman General who had been appointed Governor of Britain and, at the time of Boudicca's revolt, he was trying to gain a stronghold on the Island of Anglesey. This outcrop island in Wales was home to many British fugitives, fleeing from Roman justice, as well as many Druids. Ironically, because of the Druid's social and religious influence, (they were not only priests, but also philosophers, scientists, teachers, judges and counsellors) the Romans feared these peace-loving Celtic preachers far more than the bloodthirsty warriors.

Many of the traditional rural religious practices from the Druids have been assimilated into modern day Christianity, as it evolved to become the dominant religion in Britain. So the Druid influence survives through the many crop gathering rituals and festivals that are celebrated each year as the harvest is safely brought in. Also, more pagan rites such as the celebration of Halloween stem from Celtic origins.

Today as children happily carve Pumpkin lanterns and enjoy playing "Trick or Treat", it's hard to believe that an ancient tradition is behind all the fun and games. Although the Celts did not celebrate Halloween as we know it, they commemorated the Day of the Dead on All Hallows Day, which is the day after Halloween, the 1st of November.

But as we're just reaching the climax of Boudicca's story, it's time to stop getting sidetracked and get back to the action. During the few days that it took to reduce Colchester to ruins, a messenger had managed to reach Suetonius Paulinus, who was able to send a troop of Roman soldiers to try and assist the under-siege town. He let 5,000 of his soldiers return but Boudicca had already received word of this, and she ambushed them to the north of Colchester, wiping out the entire troop.

Boudicca then steered her victorious band of Celts towards Londinium, soon to be renamed as London and rebuilt as the new capital of the nation. This was a relatively new settlement at the time, which the Romans had founded only a decade before Boudicca's uprising. It's said that approximately 10,000 people were living there, and it expanded at great speed, quickly nearing the size of the present City of London, although the streets were about 16 feet lower than they are today. Of course, in those days there were no famous landmarks like Big Ben, Tower Bridge, Nelson's Column, the Houses of Parliament, or Westminster Abbey. Londinium wasn't even as magnificent as Colchester had been before it had been reduced to red rubble. Can you imagine today's London compared to the Londinium of yesterday; it would've been a lot like the reconstruction of the Iron Age villages we've been talking about, with a few more up market Roman Villas scattered about.

Today if you watch all the hustle, bustle and noise of the busy streets of London, complete with red Double Decker buses and black taxicabs, and the shining lights of the West End theatres, restaurants and coffee houses, imagine it all melting away into the green, open countryside of Roman-occupied Londinium, with the majestic trees, the furrowed fields and the rolling hills of Boudicca's time.

As news spread that Colchester was no more and that Boudicca was on the rampage marching on Londinium, the governor, Suetonius Paulinus, had managed to return with his troops to this relatively simple settlement before the arrival of the warrior Queen and her Army of Celts. However, never one to underestimate his opposition, the military tactician decided that he didn't have enough manpower to defend London from the passionate Celts who were determined to regain their homeland. So, unlike many other Roman commanders whose pride and ego got in the way of a sensible decision, he chose to make a tactical withdrawal before Boudicca arrived. The Roman historian, Tacitus, wrote this of the strategy of the Roman commander:

> *"He decided to sacrifice the one town to save the general situation."*

Meanwhile, Boudicca and her Army had marched through Essex destroying Roman settlements wherever they found them along the way, brutally leaving a trail of bloody mayhem behind them, as Londinium came into view. If anything, the Celts wrath hadn't been appeased in any way shape or form by the destruction of Colchester, and another Roman historian notes that the violence, torture and atrocities were equal to anything the Roman occupiers had inflicted on the Ancient Britons.

Warfare is never pretty, and historical records can be prejudiced by those who write them, in this case the Romans, but the Celts practice of mutilating bodies and hoisting them on stakes as a warning to any Romans who might stand in their way was particularly barbaric. However, these were violent times and human life was cheap and beset with danger even in peacetime. And on that gruesome note we return to our journal.

Boudicca burnt Londinium to the ground as a raging fire tore through the streets, just as she had destroyed Colchester. Again, the melted remains turned into a layer of red clay, sometimes 10 inches thick, the same 'Boudiccan Destruction Layer' that you can see in Colchester. But Boudicca and her band of warriors were still not finished.

As you look around London today, it's often difficult to spot remnants of the past, unless you happen to be a fully qualified historian; however, one of the best things about Britain's capital city for modern day visitors happens to be the amazing museums that tell the story of ancient times. The British Museum on Great Russell Street has a huge collection of artefacts from the age in which Boudicca fought her battles, including jewelry from the Iceni tribe. It even has the head of the Emperor Claudius, the Roman leader responsible for the occupation of Britain in the first place.

Well, it's the head off a statue of him that stood in front of his Temple in Colchester, and we now know what Boudicca did to that building. With her army behind her, she ripped the statue down, decapitated it, and threw the head into the nearby river. It was some 2000 years later that it was recovered and brought here for safekeeping.

Once her work was complete in London, Boudicca and her Army forged ever onwards, targeting the town of Verulamium, today's town of St Albans, as their next destination. However, news of Boudicca's advance was also spreading equally fast, and the people of Verulamium realised that they were going to be the warrior Queen's next victims. Consequently, when Boudicca arrived, with her followers now numbering over two hundred thousand, the town was completely deserted. Nevertheless, Boudicca destroyed Verulamium, evidently reluctant to stop while on a winning streak.

By this stage in the campaign Boudicca and her Celtic Army must have been feeling that they had the Romans on the run, and as they ventured northwards to confront Suetonius Paulinus face-to-face, confidence must have been extremely high. However, the Romans were not great empire builders for nothing, and he had managed to meet up with two Roman armies marching into Wales, swelling his Army to over 10 thousand soldiers. It was still nowhere near the quarter of a million rebels that Boudicca was controlling, so Paulinus was anxious to find a battlefield where he could fully exploit the Ancient Briton's weaknesses with the discipline of his Roman legions.

What happened next was a great battle and although there is disagreement about where it took place, the consensus is that both sides met at a little village called Mancetter, in Warwickshire, along Watling Street, which was the longest and most important of the incredibly straight roads that the Romans built, stretching from Dover through to London in the Southeast of England to Anglesey in the North of Wales.

The name 'Mancetter' means 'the place of chariots' and it was the site of a Roman fort too, and this is where the finale of this great historical saga was destined to be played out.

Today any hint of there being a battlefield here is long gone, as the flat, open plain of the countryside, with the River Anker running through it, is situated to the south-east of the town of Atherstone, Warwickshire, between the continually busy A5 road, which still follows the line of the Roman Watling Street, and what's known locally as the Hartshill Ridge.

Suetonius Paulinus had chosen his location well and despite Boudicca's army's superior numbers they were no match for the Roman military machine. Unfortunately, this is where Boudicca met her downfall. Although the Celts fought with passion and belief, they were destroyed by the Warrior Queen's Roman nemesis.

Imagine the scene: Wagonloads of Celtic spectators, mostly women and children, and the spoils of war, gathered from the sacking of Colchester, London and St Albans, placed behind the Army on the battlefield, ready to watch the ultimate show down.

Boudicca made an impassioned speech to rally her followers before they charged into the fray:

> *"It is not as a woman descended from noble ancestry, but as one of the people that I am avenging lost freedom, my scourged body, the outraged chastity of my daughters. Roman lust has gone so far that not our very person, nor even age or virginity, are left unpolluted. But heaven is on the side of a righteous vengeance; a legion that dared to fight has perished; the rest are hiding themselves in their camp or are thinking anxiously of flight.*
>
> *They will not sustain even the din and the shout of so many thousands, much less our charge and our blows. If you weigh well the strength of the armies, and the causes of the war, you will see that, in this battle, you must conquer or die. This is a woman's resolve; as for men, they may live and be slaves."*

The Ancient Britons charged the Romans, only to be met with a flurry of javelins, which disorientated the Celts, and then the Romans advanced as one unit, hidden by shields, as they pushed forward, stabbing and trampling all those in their path. Boudicca was cornered, as she couldn't tell her Army to retreat and re-group because they were trapped by the line of their own wagons behind them. They were armed with long swords that needed space to swing and connect, but they were crushed in a melee of their own making, because of the large Celtic Army they had accumulated, and consequently the brave warriors were unable to move.

In contrast to the disciplined, well-trained soldiers of the Roman army, Boudicca's rebels were a disorganized rabble, hindered by vast numbers of women and children, armed with swords, spears and knives. Before long Boudicca's advantage in numbers had been cancelled out and there was, quite literally, nowhere to run.

At the end of the bloody battle, 80 thousand of Boudicca's warriors had been killed, including the women and children who were waiting in the wagons behind the battle lines, while only 400 Romans lost their lives.

And what of Boudicca, the great Warrior Queen, did she survive the last battle? Reports are varied and conflicting on this subject, but whether she escaped and fled back to the Iceni country of East Anglia, or she was taken prisoner by Suetonius Paulinus, one thing is always consistent, namely that she took her own life. Wherever they were fighting in the world, it was the tradition for the leaders of the Roman's vanquished foes to be shipped back to Rome, where they would be paraded in chains through the streets, the ultimate humiliation, before being executed.

Boudicca had certainly been a worthy adversary and she would have suffered this fate without a doubt if she hadn't taken such drastic action. For a Celt, suicide was an honourable death, and wherever her remains lie, the legend of Boudicca, although lacking a happy ending, can at least boast a satisfactory conclusion. Despite Boudicca not living to see it, the Romans eventually left

Britain and the pages of history closed on this chapter of occupation. Yet this is far from being the end of the Boudicca story.

Ironically as the dark ages descended upon Britain, Boudicca vanished into the backwaters of history for many centuries. It wasn't until the Renaissance that her story was rediscovered in Roman manuscripts, most notably in the writings of Tacitus.

The Renaissance is usually considered to have originated in the late 13th Century in Northern Italy and extends to the mid 15th Century across Europe. It was the rebirth of the ideals of Classical Ancient Greece and more importantly, Rome.

However, the true resurrection of this Warrior Queen didn't take place until the 19th Centiry when Queen Victoria became Britain's sovereign in 1837. As the word 'Boudicca' translates as the Celtic word for 'Victory', and through Roman Latin translation, becomes 'Victoria', so Queen Victoria became associated with her namesake from the Ancient Britons.

For Queen Victoria there were few women that she could look back on in history that offered inspiration for a female fighting for supremacy, in a male dominated world. Queen Elizabeth I had ruled magnificently, but she came terrifyingly close to losing her life for her beliefs on several occasions, and she had also needed to bear the burden of sovereignty alone. When Queen Victoria lost her beloved husband Prince Albert, she too was alone, and a fascination with the long dead British Queens, Elizabeth and Boudicca would have been inevitable, and where Queen Victoria led, the rest of the population followed.

In London today you will see many statues of Queen Victoria, and if you know where to look, you'll find Boudicca as well.

As written earlier, there are some that believe Boudicca's last battle did not take place in Warwickshire, but instead in London. A rumor started in 1937, by an expert in mythology and Celtic folklore, stated that Queen Boudicca's body was buried under the site of Platforms 10 and 11 at King's Cross Station, London. In this version of events this wouldn't have been far from where the final show down between the great Warrior Queen and Suetonius Paulinus took place.

However, it should be stated that the strongest evidence in favor of this version of events is the existence of London's "Battle Bridge Road", which does perhaps seem a little flimsy.

But if you want to find Boudicca in London today you need to travel to the embankment of the River Thames. Her bronze statue, sculpted by Thomas Thornycroft, depicts her in a War Chariot with her daughters riding beside her, and she stands majestically next to the north end of Westminster Bridge and the Houses of Parliament. The statue was commissioned by Prince Albert, Queen Victoria's husband, before his untimely death at the age of 42 of typhoid fever. It's a magnificent commemoration of one of Britain's greatest female leaders, and standing so close to the Houses of Parliament, there are some who liken Britain's first female Prime Minister Margaret Thatcher to Boudicca, as there are few others who have made such a public show of strength against all the odds. Its only now in the 21st Century that women are beginning to enjoy the kind of equality with their male counterparts, that Boudicca as a Celt experienced, so who can say how many budding Boudicca's are out there waiting for their finest hour?

Boudicca has continued since the Victorian era to be the inspiration for copious quantities of songs and stories, with the Warrior Queen making many appearances in music and literature. And as the struggle for equality between the sexes is ongoing, she will no doubt remain in the public eye as an inspirational role model for battling women everywhere.

Yet as our journal draws to a close and we all cry "hurrah for Boudicca" we must remember that there are two sides to every story.

Under her leadership some of the most barbaric acts of reprisal were carried out against those that were innocent of any crime, just as Boudicca's own daughters had been. The Roman women who were captured suffered the worst treatment of all on the orders of Boudicca, so there was little empathy for a universal sisterhood.

In truth we must accept that although Boudicca is perceived as a symbol of women's liberation, this is in fact a distortion of history. It's so easy to look back into that past and judge the actions of our ancestors by the standards of the present. Boudicca belonged to a Celtic culture that didn't discriminate against women; she simply was fighting for survival just like her male counterparts.

Those who wish to portray her as a heroine have conveniently forgotten Boudicca's barbaric behavior. Many of the great heroes from history have also been treated in the same way. A prime example is Alexander the Great, who for many admirers is the greatest hero the world has ever known.

He probably treated his horse kindlier than any human unfortunate enough to be in his vicinity, and as absolute power, again, corrupted absolutely, his despotism ended up knowing no bounds. So just remember as you stand before the majestic statue of Boudicca, don't take everything you hear about this remarkable lady at face value.

If you need confirmation of this, all you must do is go back to her name, which today we pronounce as Boudicca. However, for anyone reading this journal who was born before 1960 as per my school years, Boadicea is the only way to pronounce this Warrior Queen's name.

So, I hear you ask, is this due to a fashion trend or a great archaeological discovery unearthed during an excavation in Iceni Country? No, it's neither of these things. The most likely explanation is that when some medieval scribe was laboring over making a copy of Tacitus's historical Roman manuscript, he made a spelling mistake, and that's probably all there is to it. Form your own opinions about Boudicca, and don't let historical prejudice sway you.

And now our time journeying into the dim and distant past to discover the identity of Boudicca, Bonduca, or even Boadicea if you prefer, really is at an end. Hopefully you'll have enjoyed the tale that forged the character of this truly remarkable Celt, who just happened to be a woman. This is one adventure into the past that truly can be described as Herstory rather than History, just for a change.

LIAM DALE

ARTHUR: KING AND COUNTRY

590AD

Tintagel, Cornwall, England on a wild and windy day is a spectacular place to be, however, for anyone with an interest in King Arthur, Tintagel is far more than a dramatic landscape. Search the history books and you'll struggle to find any reference made to England's best loved King, yet make your way to this craggy outcrop, where the sound of the sea is simply mesmerizing, and you'll find yourself closer to the legend of King Arthur than in any other place on earth.

There are those who consider Tintagel to be the site of King Arthur's court at Camelot, but for most, Tintagel is generally recognized as the place where Arthur was born. As you begin to uncover the story of Arthur's entrance into the world, you will quickly understand why he's absent from the "factual" records of history.

Our tale is set in an age when the Romans had departed Britain's shores, leaving the nation at the mercy of marauding Saxons, with a particularly bloodthirsty pair of brothers, Hengist and Horsa, leading the attack. Resisting their advances was Vortigern, a scheming opportunist who had seized power after disposing of the prince who was the rightful heir to the throne, at which point the guardians of two further Princes and heirs apparent, whisked the young boys away into hiding. Meantime Vortigern tried to appease horrible Hengist and hateful Horsa by giving them the county of Kent, but the Saxons were on the rampage and soon had added London and York to their wish list!

Quite reasonably Hengist called a peace conference with the

local nobles, but he ran true to form when he murdered every one of them who attended. Evidently slaughter suited Hengist better than democracy, although Vortigern was spared in recognition of services rendered.

Vortigern thought better of remaining in Hengist's unpredictable presence, and his alternative of location was high up in the mountains of Snowdonia in Wales. Up until this point all sounds perfectly feasible, and if you look at Vortigern's Welsh hideaway everything appears very sensible indeed, even if the names of Hengist, Horsa and Vortigern are not instantly recognisable in association with the King Arthur legend.

However, it's time for the first major twist in our tale. No matter how hard he tried, Vortigern could not construct a Castle fortress. Everyday his men would build the walls high and strong, but every night the structure would tumble down to the ground and lie in ruins. With no available explanation for things quite literally going bump in the night, Vortigern called in a team of soothsayers who soon worked out a solution.

What was required was a boy, not fathered by a mortal man, who was to be slaughtered for his blood, to be sprinkled onto the stones so that the castle would stay standing. Such a commodity was of course in very short supply, and the "dying" part of the job description was, to say the least, rather off putting. Incredibly a boy came forward, with a name that every Arthur enthusiast will instantly recognise. He was none other than Merlin, who would in years to come faithfully serve King Arthur as magician, councillor, teacher and friend.

Which means, quite evidently, that Merlin did not die on the side of a Welsh mountain, and his wise handling of the situation was a fitting prelude for what was to follow.

Merlin looked carefully at the pile of stones and informed Vortigern that spilling his blood would serve no useful purpose, as the problem lay deep beneath the castle's foundations. In an underground lake there were two dragons, one red and one white, constantly fighting, which was the reason for the nightly demolition. Intrigued, Vortigern spared Merlin's life, but in return asked the boy wizard to interpret exactly what the battling dragons meant.

What Merlin had to say was hardly music to Vortigern's ears as the red dragon represented the native Ancient Britons, whilst the white dragon was the Saxon invader. Although the white dragon was winning at that moment, the red dragon would eventually overcome to reign victorious. Unfortunately, there was no future for Vortigern as the two princes in hiding had grown up and were on their way back to avenge his murder of their older brother.

Aurelius the elder of the two princes was crowned King and he tracked Vortigern down to Monmouth Castle in South Wales. The castle was burned to the ground with Vortigern inside and the Saxon collaborator was no more. Hengist was also soon despatched to his maker by King Aurelius, and Horsa, along with the rest of the Saxons, was driven out of Britain, back across the North Sea. Merlin's prophecy had been fulfilled.

This was an age when being a King was a very dangerous business indeed and Aurelius despite having the magician Merlin at his side was murdered by an assassin. And so, it was, by right of succession, that Uther Pendragon, brother of Aurelius and father of Arthur, became King of England.

Uther was a brave warrior, but ruthless when it came to get what he wanted! Our story now leads us back to Tintagel the scene of Uther's most notorious conquest. The beautiful Igrayne was wife to Gorlious another brave warrior, until Uther fell hopelessly in love with her. Gorlious wanted to keep his wife safely out of Uther's grasp, so he brought her to Tintagel, where she could be guarded around the clock.

The narrow causeway leading out to what's known as the Island, where Tintagel Castle stood, was the only way that Uther could get to Igrayne, which meant the lovely lady was completely out of reach. That was of course until Merlin was called in to assist. With Gorlious conveniently away waging war elsewhere, Merlin created a magic potion that would transform Uther to look exactly like Gorlious. It was the perfect disguise and Uther walked straight past the guards and into the arms of the unsuspecting Igrayne.

It doesn't take too much imagination to work out that this is how the great King Arthur was conceived, but as always in cases of myth and legend, nothing was quite as straightforward as it seemed. Very usefully Gorlious was killed in battle and when Uther presented himself to Igrayne, the couple were married just before Arthur was born.

The date of this Royal birth is generally thought to have been around 475 AD, but the somewhat peculiar circumstances of Arthur's arrival does explain the lack of any historical documentation. Also, Merlin had demanded a high price for his magical love potion, claiming the first-born child of this union as his prize, and when Arthur was just a mere babe in arms he was handed over to Merlin here at Tintagel to be raised by the watchful magician.

For true historians, this is of course a fanciful tale, and visitors to Tintagel Castle today, will find ruins that date back to the early 13th Century, long after Arthur's time.

However, who can say what lies beneath the spectacular remains, where archaeological excavations have already unearthed much earlier relics and artefacts, which will undoubtedly be added to in the future.

Merlin took his "in loco parentis" responsibilities very seriously indeed, especially as Uther died when Arthur was still a young boy. The Saxon threat had certainly abated during Aurelius and Uther's reign, but it had never gone far away. Uniting the disparate tribes and clans of ancient Britain was a tough enough job and keeping the Saxon's at bay only added to the enormity of the task. Putting a child on the throne, no matter what his ancestry, would be disastrous, and knowledge of Arthur's existence would make the feuding nobles search him out to either seize control through the boy, or kill him.

Wisely Merlin entrusted the care of Arthur to a noble knight by the name of Sir Ector, who was not told who the boy was. Arthur grew into a fine young man, and just like his foster family, was completely unaware that he was the rightful King of all the land.

Celebrating Christmas as we do today owes much to the Victorian era, but back in the dim and distant dark ages, the midwinter festival of Christmas was equally as significant. For Merlin it was a perfect opportunity to present King Arthur to his people, but it would prove to be a far from easy event to stage-manage. The wise magician knew that Arthur would need to prove himself worthy from the outset if he was to stand any chance of survival, and like all good manipulators Merlin had the perfect plan in mind.

Mention the name of King Arthur and the image of the sword in the stone is never far behind and this was the crux of Merlin's great master plan! When all the nobles gathered for a Christmas church service, outside a sword miraculously appeared lodged firmly in a stone, although in some accounts it's a blacksmith's anvil. The challenge was simply this: whoever could pull the sword from the stone was the true and rightful King of England, and many tried with all their might, but failed miserably.

Eventually the nobles were called to order as the archbishop of all the land decreed that God would send them a King when the time was right. A tournament and great feast were announced for New Year's Day, when would-be monarchs could once again attempt to pull the sword from the stone.

News travelled fast and people came from far and wide to try their luck, including Sir Ector and his son Kay, with young Arthur tagging along for the ride.

Quite by chance Arthur was sent to fetch a sword for Kay and spotting the fine specimen in the stone pulled it out, knowing nothing of the reason for the sword's being there. The uproar that followed was understandable. How could this youthful lad be the right and true King of England? It was just too much for the expectant masses to take on board, after all they'd been waiting for a mighty statesman, or at the very least a grown up to govern them! Arthur put the sword back and pulled it out again, many, many times, whilst nobody else could budge it an inch. By the time Merlin appeared to announce that Arthur was indeed the son of Uther Pendragon, there was no doubt that the young man before them was the once and future King that the entire country had been waiting for.

So, we have a young King, a mighty sword, knights, tournaments and a fair scattering of damsels in distress thrown in for good measure! Not to mention of course a wily old magician on hand to direct proceedings.

This truly is the Middle Ages personified, post the Norman Conquest of 1066 and onwards, which historically speaking is some five hundred years plus after the supposed birth of Arthur. When you are going so far back in time you do expect a degree of variation, but this is quite significantly anachronistic; however, there is an explanation.

Our tale moves to the Welsh border town of Monmouth, where a resourceful 12th Century Bishop named Geoffrey, literally rewrote history. Geoffrey of Monmouth chronicled the adventures of the Celtic king Arthur, but as there were few facts to go on, he filled in any blank spaces with some imaginative supposition contemporary to his own time rather than Arthur's.

The resulting medieval hero was a big hit when Geoffrey's "History of the King's of Britain" was published and because there were few better-educated scholars to suggest otherwise, Geoffrey's version of events was accepted as accurate.

The knock-on effect was remarkable; centuries later Sir Thomas Malory's Morte D'Arthur told the story of Arthur as laid down in Geoffrey of Monmouth's history, and as it was published by William Caxton as one of the first books to come off his printing press, the myth was perpetuated for future generations. The evolutionary process continued to gather pace and by the time the great Victorian poet, Alfred Lord Tennyson came up with his version of events, nobody the whole world over could visualise King Arthur as anything but a medieval knight, and it's a tradition that continues to this very day. We all understand perfectly well that King Arthur didn't actually belong to this romantic period of history, but there's no way we'll ever give up the illusion, however much fact the historians come up with.

Selectively taking the best bits from all these sources down through the ages has created a larger-than-life character, albeit with some basis in fact, who has far more appeal than a living, breathing Celtic warlord, who may or may not have existed. You can visit the locations on the King Arthur trail, they are real enough, but what you'll find set out before you, will never allow the truth to get in the way of a very good story.

England's new young King, with Merlin on hand to guide him, built a court around himself, which had the magical name of Camelot.

Just uttering the word Camelot creates images of turreted castles, beautiful ladies, fine horses and brave knights, but even in our more recent history Camelot came to represent all things glorious and romantic once more when John F Kennedy became president of The United States of America in the 1960s. Like Arthur's Camelot, Kennedy's modern version was sparkling, vivacious but tragically short-lived; however, the impact was equally as far reaching.

Now we all know that the heart of Kennedy's Camelot was 1600 Pennsylvania Avenue, more commonly addressed as the White House, but when it comes to tracking down King Arthur's Camelot the task is considerably more complicated.

Winchester in England is a truly beautiful city which has its roots way back in Saxon times, but many believe it dates back even further, and it's certainly a contender for Arthur's Camelot.

Winchester's Great Hall is all that remains of the city's once majestic castle. During the English Civil War of the 1600s it was a Royalist stronghold, but when Oliver Cromwell rampaged through the city, victorious, he did his level best to wipe the superior castle off the face of the earth. Fortunately, the Great Hall was very useful to Cromwell as an administrative base, and it remained in use as a court of law until the late 20th Century.

If you step inside the Great Hall, you'll immediately see why thousands of King Arthur enthusiasts make their way to Winchester. Here hangs the legendary round table, where Arthur held court with not one of the knights sitting in a more favourable position than any other. It is a crucial element in the story, and at first glance at least, visitors could be forgiven for thinking that they'd stumbled upon the greatest of Arthurian relics.

Now displayed on the wall, this table would once have been supported on a pedestal and legs for a great King to sit at, but sadly it would not have been Arthur.

Thanks to modern carbon dating technology we can be certain

that King Edward 1st was responsible for building this table and even back in the 13th Century, when he was busy fighting William Wallace, the Scottish braveheart, he was one of the earliest self-confessed Arthur fanatics.

But there's a far more romantic explanation of how the round table came to be related to King Arthur when you turn to legend rather than the history books.

It's well known that a good King needs a fine Queen and Arthur was no exception. Just like his father before him, Arthur fell head over heels in love with a beautiful girl when he first laid eyes upon her, and Merlin was yet again prevailed upon to arrange matters. The young lady's name was Guinevere, but Merlin was reluctant to give his blessing, because he knew the couple were doomed to unhappiness. Yet Arthur was not to be put off and when he insisted that he would marry only Guinevere, Merlin went to her father Leodegrance and the marriage took place.

As a wedding gift Leodegrance gave Guinnevere a round table plus 100 knights to take to Arthur's court at Camelot where the principles of courage, honour, dignity and chivalry were becoming ever more important. However, whether Winchester was their destination must be debatable.

For many people the ancient county of Somerset is synonymous with King Arthur and the hill fort of Cadbury Castle, although perhaps not the most famous of Arthurian locations is a fascinating option for Camelot. Since Tudor times local folklore has claimed this to be the site of Camelot and Arthur's name is very familiar in the district. Yet it's Cadbury Castle's near neighbour, Glastonbury, that's much better known for its Arthurian connections.

Glastonbury Abbey, although a ruin, is a beautiful, deeply spiritual place, whatever it is pilgrims have come here searching for. Special Church services are still held here, and in the summer months the delightful, vaulted shrine, dedicated to Joseph of Arimathea is a favorite venue.

Long before there was any hint of Arthurian legend at Glastonbury, Joseph of Arimathea made his presence here equally as memorable. Some claim that Joseph was the uncle of Mary, the mother of Jesus, and it has even been suggested that the boy Jesus came with Joseph to Glastonbury as a child. However, it's events after the death of Jesus that connect Joseph of Arimathea most closely with Glastonbury.

According to the gospel of St Matthew, Joseph asked Pontius Pilot for permission to bury the body of Christ in his own tomb, which was granted and of course the rest is history.

After the resurrection Joseph travelled as a missionary, arriving in Britain early in the first century AD. At that time the sea reached as far inland as Glastonbury, so this is factually feasible, and Joseph brought with him a staff grown from Christ's crown of thorns, which as he struck it into Glastonbury ground, took root and flowered. Today you'll find several Holy thorn trees in the area thanks to this great legend. However, Joseph carried with him an even greater holy relic, which dramatically ties in with the King Arthur legend.

Joseph was trusted with the safe keeping of the Holy Grail, the chalice used by Christ at the last supper, and used to catch the blood of Christ at the crucifixion, which he brought here to Glastonbury.

Just a short distance from the Abbey on route towards Glastonbury Tor you'll come across the Chalice Well and gardens. This would have been a sacred site long before Joseph arrived as it was used by the Druids, and to this day the peaceful sanctuary is associated with health and wellbeing. It would have been an ideal spot for Joseph to bury the Holy Grail and it's said that the reddish color of the spring water is due to the blood of Christ.

Whatever your own thoughts, it's a wonderful, tranquil place and of course would also explain King Arthur and his knights arriving in the district as the quest for the Holy Grail was of great significance to them. It's also interesting to note that William Blake's epic poem "Jerusalem" may well allude to this incident.

> *"And did those feet in ancient time,*
> *Walk upon England's mountains green?"*
> *Could the feet have belonged to Joseph of Arimathea? After all what more appropriate location could there be than Glastonbury's green and pleasant land to keep secure the Holy Grail?*

A more tangible link to King Arthur can be found next to where the great Abbey's High Alter would once have stood. There is a small, simple plaque marking the tomb of King Arthur and Queen Guinevere where literally thousands of visitors, year in, year out, arrive to see the final resting place of Arthur.

Sadly, we can be pretty sure that whoever's bones are interned here beneath the blue of an English sky, it's unlikely to be Arthur. Monks at the Abbey found the remains in 1191, along with a lead cross complete with convenient identifying inscription. King Edward I, as we already know from evidence at Winchester was fascinated by Arthur, and even attended the re-dedication of the body in the Abbey in 1278. Cynics will point out that the monks did very nicely out of the publicity and pilgrims brought great wealth and prosperity to Glastonbury, but not all monarchs were quite as helpful to the cause.

For many hundreds of years, the grave was lost under piles of rubble because King Henry VIII destroyed the Abbey in the dissolution of the monasteries. It was only during excavations in 1934 that the Arthurian legend was re-kindled when the grave was uncovered and restored to its former glory.

Although Glastonbury has as much reason to be Camelot as any other location, it's far more likely to have been the lovely Isle of

Avalon, where water and land once met and souls of the dead passed over to another world, and we need to head back to the Arthur legend to find out more.

King Arthur was of course thrilled with the sword in the stone, which many people refer to as Excalibur, but this is not the whole story. Very early on in his Kingly career Arthur broke the sword from the stone in battle with Sir Pellinore in an ancient forest close to Camelot. Merlin's solution was to transport Arthur to a lake where a beautiful lady appeared to guide the young King to where his new sword, Excalibur was emerging from the shimmering waters. Forged in the enchanted land of Avalon, the sword had magical properties. In Arthur's hand alone, no enemy could stand against its stroke, but this was only for Arthur's lifetime, because at the hour of his death it was to be returned to the lady of the lake.

When you start to explore the majestic Glastonbury Tor, with St Michael's Tower at the summit it isn't difficult to imagine this as a mystical land. Even though there's not a drop of water in sight today, the sea once washed right up to the foot of the Tor, until it subsided leaving a beautiful lake here for many centuries. Could this have been the Isle of Avalon, so famous from the Arthurian legend? If Camelot was truly at Cadbury just a short distance away, then the pieces of the jigsaw fit.

But just as the legend of King Arthur starts to make historical and geographical sense, further research into the stories of Excalibur and the lady of the lake will lead you on a nationwide Arthurian trail with the mountains of Wales, volcanoes of Scotland and wild moors of Cornwall all demanding that their claims are heard.

Cornwall is rightly proud of its King Arthur tradition and anyone looking for a Cornish Lady of the lake and watery depths for the sword Excalibur to be returned to, will sooner or later be directed to Bodmin Moor.

Steeped in folklore from all ages past, Bodmin has a unique character that can strike terror into the heart of the bravest soul and for those in search of Excalibur's final resting place, their first port of call will be Jamaica Inn, high up on the moors. Dark and moody, this world-famous hostelry inspired by Daphne Du Maurier's magnificent novel of the same name is now quite a tourist attraction, particularly through the summer months. Tales of old smugglers, highwaymen and barbaric wreckers abound, and on a dark night it's not difficult to imagine all manner of ghostly apparitions in the atmospheric courtyard and buildings. However, for those on the King Arthur Trail, Jamaica Inn is merely a convenient landmark to help locate the romantically named Dozemary Pool.

Setting off down a winding country lane, Dozemary Pool is just a mile or so south of Jamaica Inn. There is something peacefully magical about this place, Cornwall's largest inland lake set in a gentle dip 1,000 feet above sea level.

This is a perfect example of legends converging, because there are still people today who believe Dozemary Pool to be a bottomless lake, so what better place could there be for the lady of the Lake and Excalibur to reside? But another great local myth also focuses on Dozemary Pool, albeit many centuries after King Arthur's demise.

Our time is the 17th Century, ironically an age when witchcraft and magic was as predominant in England as it was in Merlin's Day. Many folks were persecuted as witches, tried and executed in an atmosphere of fear when even a midwife going about her daily duties could be accused of witchcraft. At St Breock's Church, a short distance from Dozemary Pool, a local villain by the name of Jan Tregeagle donated vast amounts of cash so that the men of God here would fight the Devil "Faustus" style for his soul.

Satan and his hellhounds agreed that Tregeagle's soul would be spared if he toiled eternally, and the task was to empty the bottomless Dozemary Pool with a perforated limpet shell. However, should he cease his labours the Devil could claim Tregeagle's soul as a prize. There is no mention of Excalibur being found, which is hardly surprising when you consider the lake draining properties of a perforated limpet shell.

Eventually after the Devil had bombarded Dozemary Pool with thunder, lightning, earthquakes and torrential rain, Tregeagle fled to Roche Rock in the South with the hellhounds in hot pursuit and local ghost hunters claim to have encountered his evil ghost at both locations.

On a fine day it's hard to imagine Dozemary Pool as a hot bed of supernatural activity, but on a dark stormy night when the wreckers and smuggler's ghosts tread softly on the cobbles at Jamaica Inn, you might just encounter the spirit of Tregeagle and the hellhounds at Dozemary Pool, along with a phantom King Arthur, his faithful Knight Sir Bedevere and of course the lady of the lake to complete the full set.

Remembering that Somerset had the logical claim of Camelot at Cadbury Castle and the Isle of Avalon at Glastonbury, what logical progression of the King Arthur legend could possibly point to the far off the beaten track Dozemary Pool, high up on Bodmin Moor?

King Arthur and Queen Guinevere presided at court, with the knights performing great feats of daring, as the golden age of Camelot shone brightly. Sir Gawain did battle with the Green Knight and the pure Sir Galahad took on the quest for the Holy Grail, but the light of Camelot was dimming as Merlin's predictions for the marriage of Arthur and Guinevere proved correct.

Family feuds have throughout history given us some of the most fascinating tales, and in Arthur's case the treachery of a relation struck a fatal blow. There are those who believe that Sir Mordred was Arthur's nephew, whist others with more of a taste for Royal scandal suspected him to be Arthur's son from an incestuous liaison with his half-sister. Whatever the truth, the other knights warned Arthur about Mordred, but the King refused to listen, and it cost him dearly!

But Mordred wasn't Arthur's only problem. The brave and handsome Sir Lancelot had taken the fancy of the Queen, and the pair fell head over heels in love. Whether they were lovers in the true sense or not is incidental as Mordred went to Arthur and told him that Guinevere had committed adultery with Lancelot, the King's "First Knight".

This was enough to set Arthur into a jealous frenzy, pursuing Lancelot countrywide and even the brave Knight's stronghold at Bamburgh Castle in Northumberland, Northern England could offer no protection. Meantime Guinevere was sentenced to death, by burning at the stake, for high treason, and was only rescued in the nick of time by Lancelot as the flames were flickering at her feet.

Mordred had achieved his goal. Camelot was in disarray and with Arthur chasing Lancelot and Guinevere, some say as far as France, the black hearted Mordred was able to make a very hostile takeover bid.

One of the greatest legends from this episode concerns one of South Cornwall's most dramatic attractions, the serenely beautiful St Michael's Mount. It was here that Arthur stopped off enroute to France to slay a Giant that was terrorising the district. Today the Island is cut off from the mainland at high tide, but the landscape would probably have looked very different in Arthur's day.

Heading ever southward from Penance, the closest town to St

Michael's Mount, travelers will inevitably run out of road as they reach, quite literally, Land's End.

Here the crashing waves will never fail to impress and as you gaze out to sea the legend of the lost land of Lyonesse takes on a new resonance all of its own. The Scilly Isles lie some 30 miles south of Land's End and Lyonesse was said to be the peninsula of land that joined the two locations. St Michael's Mount could well have been part of Lyonesse and with its verdant woodland at the summit it could well have been a fine hideaway for a giant.

Lyonesse was a land of great fertility inhabited by a beautiful race who constructed fine cities and as many as 140 magnificent churches. Guinevere has often been linked with Lyonesse, as the land of her birth, and there are also claims that Arthur fought his final, fatal battle with Mordred on Lyonesse. This would of course make Dozemary Pool very logical for the disposal of Excalibur.

The story goes that a mighty flood wiped out Lyonesse more than 900 years ago. Sleeping people were drowned and all but the very highest peaks were engulfed. On stormy nights there are still reports of the church bells of Lyonesse ringing out and generations of Mount's Bay fishermen have told tales of seeing the submerged roofs of houses beneath the still waters on clear, bright moonlit nights. This truly is a delightful legend, and it would take a very unromantic soul not to get caught up in the myths and magic of Lyonesse on a visit to Land's End.

To add an extra twist to the King Arthur tale, some renditions of the story of Arthur's last stand against Mordred state that Merlin appeared as the King was struck a fatal blow.

Lyonesse was lost as Merlin created a mighty tidal wave to drown Mordred's army, allowing Arthur's knights to escape, and the land was never restored. Whether act of God or act of magic, the story of Lyonesse will live on eternally as Cornwall's very own answer to the lost city of Atlantis.

The Welsh also have a very strong claim to the legend of King Arthur, not least in part due to Geoffrey of Monmouth's colorful history of the Kings of Britain.

Returning to Snowdonia, where the Celtic and Saxon dragons of Vortigern once battled, the Welsh have their own version of events.

Arthur's last battle, according to them, was fought in a narrow, mountainous pass where the treacherous Mordred and his archers ambushed the King and his knights. The dramatic scenery of the Pass of Llanberis in Snowdonia is certainly popular with visitors in search of King Arthur, and it's claimed that the mighty monarch and his brave knights lie resting on their shields in a nearby cave.

There is also conveniently a lake close at hand, where Excalibur could have been disposed of, and with Caerleon in the south of Wales providing yet another possible location for Camelot, the jigsaw pieces can undoubtedly be made to fit.

Arthur's Seat, a cannon shot from the castle, always impresses visitors to Edinburgh, a stunning wild landscape provided by an extinct volcano, slap bang in the heart of the city.

There are water features a plenty to satisfy any lady of the lake, but this location is unlikely to have had any connection with the Arthur of this tale, although it does illustrate very neatly how a legend can grow. It has been suggested that "Arthur" in this case is a derivation of the word "Archer" and the summit of this volcano would have offered any archer a fantastic vantage point.

The last battle of Arthur and the great Knight's final resting place is perhaps an even greater fascination for modern day Arthurian enthusiasts than finding the location of Camelot itself.

Turn to Thomas Malory or Lord Alfred Tennyson and the story

is equally as gripping although the actual location remains frustratingly mysterious.

As Arthur lay dying, he turned to his faithful Knight, Sir Bedivere and asked him to return the sword Excalibur to the Lady of the Lake. Now, for the Celts this would not have seemed a strange request, as it was standard practice to throw their finest metal work into lakes as an offering to the Gods. But the beauty and power of Excalibur tempted Bedivere, and it took him three attempts to do as he was asked. Then the lady of the Lake appeared in a boat draped with blackened sails to take Arthur to the Isle of Avalon.

To add to the locations already considered as possible sites for Arthur's last battle, Cornwall has a further contender at Slaughter Bridge near Camelford and a site close to Cadbury Castle in Somerset has also been suggested for obvious reasons.

But this was not the last to be heard of Arthur, and if the final battle near Cadbury Castle is a possibility, then the next part of the story will make sense.

For many centuries local folklore has been adamant that King Arthur, his brave knights and their horses lie sleeping beneath the grassy folds of Cadbury Hill, Somerset. Their ghosts have been seen down through the ages, with Midsummer's Eve proving to be the most popular time for them to walk the earth. Custom has named a nearby watering hole "Arthur's Well" and it's to that spot that the ghostly procession of knights on horseback, led by King Arthur himself slowly make their way. Local residents have even heard tell that on one occasion when the ghosts appeared, a witness to the event picked up a silver horseshoe that fell by the wayside.

No doubt this became a treasured possession indeed, but who it was and what happened to the horseshoe, just like the tales of King Arthur, have long since been consigned to the annuls of myth and legend.

Unfortunately, there's no guarantee that taking the King Arthur trail for yourself will uncover any horseshoes, or that you'll get a glimpse of an Arthurian ghost, but what you will experience is a sense of the past that really does make history come to life.

From the wild landscape of Tintagel, Arthur's birthplace, there is a sense of majesty, man pitting his wits against the elements and surviving against all the odds.

Then there's the strength of the Roman remains at Caerleon, the Great Hall at Winchester and the undulating Cadbury Castle all claiming the title of Camelot. Moving on we have the lakes, ranging from the mountains of Snowdonia to Avalon at Glastonbury and Dozemary Pool high up on Bodmin Moor. Finally, there are a multitude of proposed resting places for Arthur and his knights, and you really can take your pick, which is undoubtedly the key to each new generation's fascination with the story.

What happened to the other main protagonists also makes for interesting speculation. There are plenty of folk who believe that Merlin is alongside King Arthur and the sleeping knights, however some years earlier Merlin was tempted by a better offer from his beautiful apprentice Vivien. Sadly, for him she was as treacherous as Mordred and sealed the old magician in a tomb to die a slow and tragic death.

As for the feuding between Lancelot and Arthur, it's hard to imagine the knights of the Round Table, even in waiting, without the King's First knight. Perhaps all was restored between the two men when poor old Guinevere got sent off to a nunnery, the standard fate for all disgraced medieval heroines.

Yet for incurable romantics everywhere the legend of King Arthur brings with it a message of hope. The brave knights who lived by a chivalrous code are not dead, but only sleeping, waiting for the day that they will be called upon to protect their beloved country once more. The fact that if an "Arthur" really did exist, and take on the Saxon invaders, he would have been nothing like Malory's medieval King doesn't matter in the slightest!

This truly is the stuff of legend, and very good it is too. In times of national troubles Arthur will always boost morale. Just the thought of Camelot and all it stood for, the preservation of honour, truth and justice has made the toughest battle worth the winning, and if Arthur's present-day popularity is anything to go by, whatever the crisis Britain as a nation may face, King Arthur will constantly be a valuable weapon in any arsenal. It's no accident that authors, artists, musicians and filmmakers perpetuate the myth of Arthur on a regular basis; he has a great deal to offer the modern world. The legendary Arthur was, is and always will be a source of inspiration, for Kings and commoners alike, a chivalrous hero to shape the future, whatever the truth about King Arthur's past might prove to be.

◆ ◆ ◆

RICHARD 1ST – THE LIONHEART

1157AD

There have been some truly great Kings and Queens of England, and by equal measure several truly appalling Monarchs to have made their indelible mark on history. Many factors influence public opinion on whether a Sovereign has been good or bad, hero or villain, sinner or saint, and on just a few occasions it's difficult to make a judgement either way. This is absolutely the dilemma that surrounds King Richard the first, the Lionheart, who could transform from a brave, chivalrous Crusader Knight into a cruel despot within the space of a heartbeat.

Over time Richard the Lionheart has become a fascinating figure in Great Britain's history and his worldwide travels through lands that are still, to this very day, at the heart of global conflict, also bestow upon him an international resonance. This history journal, will set out on a journey of discovery to find the man behind the myth and explore, expand and expose the legend that is Lionheart.

Standing majestically along the banks of the River Thames, which connects Great Britain's capital city, London, to the sea, is the ornate and beautiful Palace of Westminster. This grand and ancient building is also known as the Houses of Parliament, as it is home to the House of Commons, where the democratically elected Members of Parliament sit and debate every issue of Government, and the House of Lords, where the unelected Peers of the Realm and Clerics of the Church of England discuss the new laws that their neighbouring house will pass.

The Palace of Westminster is overlooked by the equally famous Clock Tower, a giant structure which houses the Great Bell of Westminster, popularly known as 'Big Ben', which chimes regularly every hour on the hour.

However, the oldest part of the Palace of Westminster dates to the late 11th Century, when Westminster Hall was built. Inside this London landmark, underneath the world's finest, surviving hammer beam roof, is where they lay the newly departed statesmen and Royal Family members for the public to pay their last respects. People like William Gladstone in 1898 and Winston Churchill in 1965, two of Great Britain's finest Prime Ministers, and the beloved and much-missed Queen Mother, wife of King George the Sixth and mother of the present Queen, Elizabeth the second, who passed away at the amazing age of 101 in 2002.

But it's the vicinity just outside Westminster Hall that commands the attention for the tale we are about to tell. For here, in the open-air cast in the finest bronze, is the likeness of King Richard the First. He is sat astride his trusty horse, brandishing his sword as if ready to charge into battle, and demands respect even as an immovable statue. This solidified ghost of a warrior King has captured the imagination of the public like no other King before or since. He was given the title *'Coeur de Lion'*, which translates as Heart of a Lion, because of his courage and bravery in battle.

Although he could speak little English and only spent six months of his decade-long reign in the country he ruled, his short time as King of England made him more famous than any other King and firmly established him as a literary icon, appearing in swashbuckling tales of chivalrous Knights, like Sir Walter Scott's *'Ivanhoe'*, and as the focus for folk tales such as *'Robin Hood'*.

Nevertheless, to side-line King Richard the First in history, as nothing more than a so-called 'absent King' does him a grave injustice.

Richard the Lionheart was the son of King Henry of Anjou and Queen Eleanor of Aquitaine, two of the most intriguing and domineering royal characters in medieval history.

Richard's father, King Henry the Second, held several titles. He was the King of England, the Duke of Normandy, the Count of Anjou and after he married Richard's mother, Eleanor, the Duke of Aquitaine. He was also the firstborn to begin the Plantagenet dynasty, which had started with his own father, Geoffrey of Anjou. Plantagenet was a surname derived from the broom flower, which is an evergreen deciduous shrub, with slender stems, yellow flowers and small leaves, which Geoffrey of Anjou used as an emblem and a good luck charm.

Due to the way that history is on occasion sensationalised, where certain instances seem to stick in the mind more readily than others, King Henry the Second is probably most famous because of his treatment of his old religious friend Thomas a Becket, who he appointed Archbishop of Canterbury in 1162. Becket had originally been King Henry's trusted Chancellor when they worked tirelessly, side-by-side, to bring law and order to an England ravaged by internal strife, civil war and corrupt landowners.

In Medieval England, the Church held all the power. The fear of going to Hell meant that people did what the Church told them, as only the Catholic Church could save your soul and allow you to go to Heaven. The Catholic Church sent its orders from Rome, where the Pope held office. In Medieval England, the Archbishop of Canterbury was the most important position in the Church. Thomas a Becket's appointment as Archbishop was a political one, as King Henry the Second wanted the powerful Church to become the monarchy's servant.

Henry the second had established courts in various parts of England, allowing the royal practice of granting magistrates the power to render legal decisions on a wide range of civil matters in the name of the Crown, while permitting Church Courts less and less power.

At this time, the Church was morally ambivalent, in the sense that if a Bishop committed murder, he had the right to be tried in a Church court, which answered to God, rather than the monarchy. He would, by all accounts, be pardoned and allowed to continue his daily life. King Henry the Second appointed Thomas a Beckett to bring the Church into line.

Where once Becket had been loyal and faithful to the King, his consecration as Archbishop seemed to bring about a religious fervor and he became difficult and critical.

Henry's radical reform of the law proved to be one of his major contributions to the social history of England, but the Church vehemently opposed it, as any privileged power would, and found its spokesman in Thomas a Becket. Henry had appointed Becket precisely because he wanted to avoid conflict, so he had no choice but to exile his friend. Beckett fled to France where Henry's archenemy (and former husband of his wife, Eleanor), King Louis of France, was only too happy to shield Becket from the English King.

When Thomas a Becket eventually returned to England, he headed straight for the safety of Canterbury Cathedral. Canterbury is a small city in comparison to London, but the Cathedral dominates the land like a protective talisman. It stands majestic and proud, in a testament to the grand architecture of days gone by.

King Henry was known for his quick temper and aggravated and frustrated by Becket, it's alleged that in a fit of rage he yelled; *'Will no-one rid me of this turbulent priest?'* Taking this exasperated outcry as an order, four loyal Knights, Reginald Fitzurse, Hugh de Moreville, William de Tracey, and Richard le Breton, immediately plotted the murder of the archbishop, and accomplished it in front of the alter at Canterbury Cathedral on Tuesday, December the 29th, 1170, when Thomas a Becket was at prayer.

His assasination by the swords of these four knights is depicted in one of the earliest 13th Century illustrated manuscripts of the period.

Becket was singled out as a martyr by Pope Alexander of Rome and would later be canonized. King Henry had to publicly apologize and be seen to pay public penance at Becket's tomb every day.

Since Becket's death, Canterbury Cathedral has become a place of pilgrimage for millions of people, a journey immortalized in Geoffrey Chaucer's *'Canterbury Tales'*, written an incredible 600 years ago.

In contrast to the masculine power of King Henry the Second, his wife and Richard the Lionheart's mother, Eleanor of Aquitaine, was a strong advocate for the rise of feminism, centuries before the bra was invented let alone burnt. Aquitaine was a huge region in South-Western France including the town of Bordeaux, and Eleanor was raised in the most cultured court in Europe. She was highly educated for a woman of those times.

She could read, speak fluent Latin, was well versed in literature and music, as well as enjoying the outdoor pursuits of riding and hunting. When she was 15, her father died, and she became the richest and most eligible heiress in the world. Because this was at a time in history when men thought nothing of kidnapping a wealthy heiress in order to marry her and claim her money and lands, her father wrote in his will that she must be married to Prince Louis the Seventh of France, who was the heir to the French throne.

The wedding present that Eleanor gave to Louis was an expensive rock crystal vase, which is still on display in the Louvre, in Paris today. In August 1137, within days of their marriage, Prince Louis became rightful King of France when his father unexpectedly passed away. The teenage couple were the complete antithesis of each other; she was forceful, radical and flirtatious, whereas he was studious, conformist and committed.

They had two daughters together and she even accompanied him on the second of the famous Holy Crusades before, she set tongues wagging about an incestuous closeness with her uncle, Raymond of Poitiers.

In another nod to modern feminist values, Eleanor was also granted a divorce by the Pope; unheard of in medieval times, when she tired of King Louis of France as a husband. In 1152, within six weeks of her divorce, she was married to King Henry the Second of England who was 18 years her junior. She was already pregnant with their first son, William, who would only survive a few years beyond his birth. She then gave birth to Henry, Matilda, our Lionheart Richard, Geoffrey, Eleanor, Joan, and John.

Richard the Lionheart, her third and favorite child, was born on the 8th of September 1157, in the academic and intellectual town of Oxford, in England. Oxford is known as the *'City of Dreaming Spires'*, a term coined for the harmonious architecture of the university buildings. Richard was born in Beaumont Palace, which no longer exists today. However, Worcester College (founded in 1714) lies across the end of Beaumont Street and built into the stone pillar for the garden railings, there is a small plaque marking the location of Beaumont Palace. It reads:

> *'Near to this site stood the King's Houses, later known as Beaumont Palace. King Richard I was born here in 1157 and King John in 1167'*

Meanwhile, King Louis of France, after losing his wife to Henry the Second and being left with two daughters, took a succession of wives in order to try and produce a male heir to the throne of France.

Eventually, in 1165, an heir was born and christened Prince Philip Augustus the Second. This King of France-to-be would prove as significant in Richard the Lionheart's story, as his father had been in the fortunes of Henry the Second.

Richard the Lionheart grew up around his mother, Eleanor, at Court in Poitiers in France. Richard became the Duke of Aquitaine in 1172, at only fourteen-years of age. It was here that he learned how to be a Knight. He was taught to ride and to fight on horseback and entered many tournaments to improve his skills. Tournaments, in medieval times, were less about civilized one-to-one jousting, and more about learning to fight together as a unit in mock battle situations. It was Richard who during his reign as King encouraged tournaments to take place in England, where they had none, for his kingdom to be better prepared for battle if an invasion came.

The rivalry and relationships within the Plantagenet family were unhealthy and vicious. King Henry the Second decreed that, after his death, the bulk of his dominions would go to his namesake and eldest son, Henry (known as the Young King). In 1170, long before his father died, Young King Henry was crowned and given his title. This meant, effectively, that England had two Kings – both called Henry.

Meanwhile, Richard the Lionheart was promised to Princess Alice of France, the daughter of King Louis and the brother of

Prince Philip. Richard had also been given the Duchy of Aquitaine, to stop him feeling jealous of his brother, the Young King Henry, and the investment ceremony took place in Saint-Hilaire-le-Grand Church in Poitiers.

Two years later he was given the duchy of Poitiers too and was invested in the very same church again.

However, nobody was happy with these arrangements, as the three sons, Henry, Richard and Geoffrey, believed that their father gave them titles freely but wouldn't give them any authority. They were also suspicious that he would eventually pass on his lands to the youngest son, John. Their mother, Eleanor fueled by jealousy brought on by Henry's many extra-marital affairs, encouraged her sons to take what was rightfully theirs. So, in 1173, the three brothers took up arms and fought against their father in battle in order to leave the Young King Henry as the only holder of the throne in England.

In 1174, a year into the war with his father, Richard managed to secure the French town of Saintes and, in doing so, impressed his father greatly. Because of his financial resources, quicker speed and mastery of organization, Henry the Second defeated his two sons, Henry and Geoffrey, quickly and painlessly. However, Richard was the last to give in after his father tried to invade Aquitaine not once but twice, fighting for the honor of his mother's birthright, with her support. When he did bow to his father's superior forces, Henry the Second pardoned his son and was keen to make use of Richard's military brain and tactical knowledge. He did not, however, let Eleanor off so lightly. She was imprisoned and kept locked away in Chinon Castle for the remainder of Henry's life.

The victorious Henry the Second wanted the various Barons of Aquitaine, forever rebellious of English law, crushed into submission.

In 1174, he ordered Richard to take an army and lay siege to them. It was the master stepping back to see if the pupil had learnt enough to stand alone. Henry needn't have worried. Although this conflict lasted five years, it ended in victory for Richard with the destruction of the fortress of Taillebourg in 1179. This castle was inaccessible on three sides due to mountains, and the fourth side was heavily fortified. Richard knew that the overthrow of Taillebourg would lead to the immediate surrender of the Barons. Within fourteen days, Richard had secured the 'virgin fortress', as it was known, due to its impregnability, and as he predicted, this show of force and brilliance made the rest of the rebel Barons immediately surrender to his control. This victory earned Richard increasing fame and praise.

Young King Henry had become increasingly jealous of the fame and responsibility heaped upon his brother Richard in those five years. Like a good Plantagenet, he was soon plotting against him.

Richard's reign over Aquitaine led to a major revolt in 1183. The future Lionheart had a terrible reputation, causing many casualties of war. The rebels hoped to rid themselves of Richard and asked his brothers Henry and Geoffrey to help them succeed. Henry the Second feared that the conflict between his three sons could lead to the ultimate destruction of his kingdom and threw his support behind Richard. Then tragedy struck when the younger Henry died unexpectedly of dysentery, ending the revolt, and again Richard won the day.

It was at about this time in his career that Richard heard news of the re-capture of the Holy Land by the Muslim Army, after the Battle of Hattin, which set in place the foundations for a Third Crusade.

The First Crusade had begun nearly a hundred years previously, in 1095. The Holy City of Jerusalem was controlled by Turkish Muslims, who forbade Christians to worship there, even though the Christians regarded Jerusalem as their most Holy City too. In order to regain control, the Pope decided that the Christians should reclaim their Holy Land. Many different nations took up the call from the Pope and Knights were sent to fight for the cause from all over Western Europe. There was no real organised leadership, with everyone travelling over land or by sea in order to reach Jerusalem.

The sacred city was taken from the Turks in 1099, establishing the Kingdom of Jerusalem. This initial Crusade was a major turning point in the expansion of Western power, and ironically was the only crusade to achieve its stated goal. When the Pope announced to the general public that there would be a Crusade to re-capture the Holy Land, he used the famous phrase: *'God wills it!'*

However, on Christmas Eve, 1144, the frontier fortress of Edessa was captured, a town located in modern-day Turkey, which inflicted a serious blow on the Christian power base. The Pope called for a Second Crusade to free Edessa, and a combined Crusader Army of French and German forces were despatched to fight another Holy War.

In 1187, The Battle of Hattin, which instigated Richard's interest in the Crusades, took place near the Lake of Galilee and was a carefully executed plan of attack by a Muslim Leader called Al-Malik al-Nasir Salah ed-Din Yusuf. In the West, he was just known as Saladin.

A force to be reckoned with, Saladin commanded the Syrian Army as well as taking up a position as leader of all Egypt. After forcing the Crusader Army to camp for the night outside the city, Saladin's army set fire to surrounding bushes and trees in order to give the Christian soldiers a very miserable and very sleepless night. In the morning, tired and demoralised, the Crusader Army could see they were surrounded by Saladin and his men.

On a holy quest Saladin stormed city by city, taking such prizes as Jaffa and Beirut, before reaching Jerusalem, effectively extinguishing the Christian presence there.

Because Saladin wanted all his followers to recognise his leadership as a moral one, he was honest and generous when dealing with either friend or foe. Unlike modern day politicians, he kept his promises. It was this integrity that earned Saladin the admiration of his own countrymen, and the respect of his enemies.

As was characteristic of Richard the Lionheart, he decided to take the Cross, which was a vow to go on a Crusade in the form of a piece of material shaped like a cross and didn't even think about consulting his father. Henry the Second had been planning a Crusade for years but had just never got around to it, even going so far as to pass the 'Saladin Tithe' on the people of England, which was yet another form of taxation to swell the royal coffers. Taking the Cross was not only a grand gesture but also a wise business move, being as all your debts were postponed until you returned, and your property was entrusted to the Church for safekeeping. Of course, the biggest draw was that the Crusaders were granted freedom from the terrors of purgatory and Hell, as they were quite literally promised the Kingdom of Heaven.

However, Richard was held back from joining the Third Crusade because of matters at home. His father, Henry still wanted to capture Aquitaine and give it away to John, his younger brother. Richard joined forces with King Philip of France, the son of his mother's ex-husband, to issue a joint ultimatum. Richard would marry Princess Alice, the sister of Philip, and King Henry would publicly declare that Richard was the rightful and only heir to the throne of England. However, never one to do as he was bid, Henry refused, forcing Richard to pledge allegiance to France's King instead. He agreed to give away his rights to Normandy and Anjou, if King Philip of France would help him defeat Henry and his army. And that was exactly what they did.

It's often been hinted that there was more to the relationship between Richard and Philip than meets the eye. It was undoubtedly very complicated, and a homosexual liaison is certainly one possible explanation for the evident affection between the two men turning to bitter enmity during the Third Crusade. Yet there are plenty of alternatives, one being the treatment of Philip of France's sister at the hands of the Plantagenets.

The truth was that Princess Alice could not have married Richard without a great public outcry, because she was in fact already the mistress of his father Henry the Second. With divorce proceedings against Richard's mother Eleanor already being negotiated, Alice gave birth to several of Henry's illegitimate children, which would hardly have endeared either father or son to the lady's brother. Also, Richard's own despotic tendencies would have been sufficient to alienate the French King, as we will soon discover.

In 1189, King Henry the Second, already ill and dying, ended up torching Le Man, the very French village that he was born in, before surrendering to Richard and Philip whilst calling a retreat. One of his last acts before he died was to grant a pardon to all of those who had conspired against him and to declare Richard as the rightful heir to the English throne. His last hours were spent in Chinon, France, before his body was carried to Fontevraud and then laid in the choir of the abbey room.

Richard The First, the man with the heart of a Lion, was now King of England, and one of his first acts as Sovereign was to release his mother Eleanor from her 15-year imprisonment.

Richard headed for England, not out of honour and duty but in order to find twenty-four thousand marks to pay off King Philip of France for his help during the fight against Richard's father. At this time in history, for the Plantagenet Kings, England was effectively acting as a giant cash depository for France and had accumulated nearly two thousand marks for war funds.

The coronation of Richard 1st took place on Sunday, 3rdSeptember 1189, at Westminster Abbey in London. The Abbey itself was built by Edward the Confessor in the 11th Century and re-built in a suitably Gothic style in the 13th. Since Christmas Day, 1066, when William the Conqueror was crowned King of England, all reigning monarchs have been crowned in Westminster Abbey, except for Lady Jane Grey, Edward the Fifth and Edward the Eighth.

It has also been used to house Benedictine Monks throughout the years and as a place of learning. Poet's Corner is probably the most famous burial place in the entire nation being the final resting place of Geoffrey Chaucer, author of *'The Canterbury Tales'*, because he was living here at the time of his death. The honor soon spread beyond just poets and includes such famous names as Sir Isaac Newton, William Pitt the Younger, Clement Attlee, Rudyard Kipling, Thomas Hardy, Ralph Vaughan Williams and William Shakespeare.

In the writings of the time, there is a fully detailed account of this coronation, the first proper record of such a ceremony, from the 13th Century *'Chronicle of the Kings of England'*. Along a path made of woollen cloth, Richard was escorted from his chamber in the Palace of Westminster (where his bronze statue now stands) as far as the high altar of Westminster Abbey. At the head of the procession went the clergy, carrying holy water, crosses, candles and censors, chanting as they moved on. There were Priors, Abbots, Bishops and Richard's own brother, John - each of them carrying a Sword of State, which were made from solid gold. Six Barons carried the royal robes and insignia. The Earl of Essex carried the ornate golden crown, studded with priceless stones.

When he reached the high altar, Richard took the coronation

oath. He swore that he would observe peace, honor and reverence towards God and the Holy Church. He also vowed to exercise righteous justice over all the people committed to his charge and if any bad laws or evil customs had been introduced to this kingdom, he would abolish them and would enact good laws instead.

He was then stripped bare to the waist and the Archbishop of Canterbury anointed him with holy oil on his chest, hands and head. This practice happened all the way through until Queen Victoria in the 19th Century when she was just anointed on her hands and on her head. It is this act, rather than the symbolic placing of the crown, that confers upon the new ruler that his kingship is given to him through the divine sanctity of God.

The crown itself was so heavy that the crowning had to be done with two Earls holding the crown itself, to take the strain off it. It was after accepting the sceptre and the verge that Richard sat on the throne and waited for Mass to be celebrated. A single nocturnal bat fluttered around the throne during Mass, which many on-lookers took to be a bad omen, considering it was very unusual to see one flying around at midday.

Unfortunately, during the feasting the bad omen of the bat appeared to be true as Jews bearing gifts for the King were barred from entering the Palace. The Christian crowds at the gates killed some of them and wounded others. This, in turn, led to rioting in the city of London, which didn't become calm until the morning. King Richard was furious, not because he had a special affection for Jews, but because this group of people were under his protection, mainly since they were a very rich seam of income and revenue. More riots followed throughout England as the crusading spirit took over and anti-Jewish feeling prevailed.

As the newly crowned King, Richard didn't feel the need to endear himself to the people as all his thoughts were focused on raising enough capital to get to the Crusade.

He sold off everything that he could, saying that he would sell London itself if he could find anyone rich enough to buy it. Even though King Richard was born in England, the country itself held no affection in his Lion's heart.

In fact, he declared that it seemed *'bitterly cold and always raining'*. Richard like his father before him saw the country as his own personal investment fund. A tax system had been set up in England years earlier by the Anglo-Saxon Kings, which was always high, especially compared to anywhere else in Europe.

To appease his younger brother John, he gave him the title of Earl of Gloucester, as well as relinquishing control to him of whole counties such as Nottinghamshire, Derbyshire, Somerset, Dorset, Devon and Cornwall. But again, like his father before him, King Richard gave with one hand and took away with the other. He didn't want John trying to claim any right to be King of England whilst he was gone, so Richard banished John into exile for three years and appointed his mother, Eleanor, as regent in his absence.

In the month of July 1190, King Richard set off for the Crusades from Portsmouth on the south coast of England. Four years later, this was to be the home of the Royal Navy. The Dockyard has been at the forefront of technological development for over 500 years. The world's first dry dock had been built here in 1495 and it was later home to the father of Isambard Kingdom Brunel, noted architect of the Clifton Suspension Bridge in Bristol.

Marc Brunel, Isambard's father, invented the first steam powered industrial production line for the manufacture of wooden pulley blocks and it was also in the Portsmouth Dockyard that the revolutionary steam turbine powered HMS Dreadnought was built at the beginning of the 20th century. It's now the home of a wonderful museum and exhibition centre, as well as providing visitors with the sights of many different boats and ships of all ages, sizes and historical importance.

According to Richard of Devizes, a monk at Winchester at the time of Richard's reign, his Crusade to the East caused the people of England to appreciate their new King.

> "The King was indeed worthy of the name of King, for in the very first year of his reign, for Christ's sake he left the realm of England almost as if he were going away and would not return. So great was this man's devotion and thus quickly, thus speedily and hastily he ran, or, rather, flew to avenge Christ's injuries."

Richard the Lionheart joined up with King Philip of France almost immediately and the vast army of men then split in two when they reached Lyon, as food supplies from the land were no longer enough for them to journey together on the same route. King Richard's route started out from Vezelay to Lyons, then to Marseilles and through to Genoa, in Italy. Through Tuscany he went until he got to Rome, heading straight on for Naples, before reaching Messina, in Sicily. It was there that they met up again with King Philip of France's men.

Upon arrival, they were swept up in a crucial moment in Sicily's history. Following the death of King William, the Second of Sicily, there was some dispute over who was going to take the throne. His heir was an aunt called Constance who was married to a German. Nobody wanted a German King and so the Pope and the Sicilian Barons passed the crown on to Tancred of Lecce, an illegitimate cousin of their original King.

King Richard ignored the political shenanigans and attempted to keep his men trim and trained by arranging tournaments. In one such duel, the French Knight William de Barres scored such a hit on the English King that it dented his helmet. In a fit of pique, Richard counter-attacked William but fell to the ground when his saddle slipped from underneath him. He immediately summoned for a new horse and attacked again. William would not budge from his seat. With dented pride and bruised ego, King Richard ordered the brave French Knight to be sent away. It was only on the eve of their eventual departure from Sicily that Richard relented and allowed William to return to King Philip's service.

During their stay in Messina, the question of King Richard's betrothal to King Philip's sister, Princess Alice, became a major issue. His mother, Eleanor of Aquitaine, even travelled to Sicily with a new bride for her son, Berengaria, daughter of the King of Navarre. Eleanor wanted to bring peace to the southern border of Aquitaine, with the alliance of this arranged marriage. King Philip, insulted by Richard's refusal of his sister and the claims that Richard made of Alice's affair with his deceased father, Henry the Second, attempted to encourage the newly appointed King Tancred of Sicily into an alliance, in order to overpower and imprison the King of England.

Tancred made a treaty of friendship with Richard instead. This was marked by the exchanging of gifts and Richard's present to Tancred was the famous sword Excalibur, owned by the legendary King Arthur. This was since, around this time, the tombs of King Arthur and his wife the Lady Guinevere were believed to have been 'discovered' at Glastonbury. King Philip was outraged, and left Messina before Richard's new bride arrived.

Eleanor of Aquitaine, now an elderly lady of seventy, wanted to stay long enough to see her son's wedding, but the marriage was postponed because of Lent, so, she completed the long journey home to France pausing only in Rome, to visit the Pope.

Back in England, Prince John, left to his own devices without the controlling presence of his mother, Eleanor, caused merry havoc and mischief whenever visiting England and, even upon his mother's return, continued to try and usurp his brother's power as King.

King Richard, eager to set sail for the Holy Land, took his bride-to-be with him. His huge fleet of two hundred vessels set off from Messina on 10th of April 1191.

Only three days out from Messina, a storm blew through the large convoy and many ships were blown completely off course. Richard's ship guided the way forward with a burning light at the masthead but not everyone could keep pace. Upon reaching Rhodes, in Greece, he was shocked to discover that one of the ships missing was the one carrying his fiancée, Berengaria.

Fast galleys were sent out on a rescue mission to see if they could discover the whereabouts of these lost vessels. Eventually, the ship carrying Berengaria was found moored off Limassol, on the south coast of the Island of Cyprus. Some of the other off-course vessels had been run aground and anyone who reached dry land was seized, stripped of all their possessions, and then thrown into prison.

Limassol was built between two ancient cities, Amathus and Kourion, and the ruins of Kourion are extensive and include well-preserved mosaics. To the west of the city is the Akrotiri, Sovereign Base Area of the United Kingdom, a leftover from the days of the rule of Richard the Lionheart. This allows the island to run as an independent state but aids in defence, foreign affairs and trade issues.

Back in Medieval times, Cyprus was an island famous for its vineyards and had long been a cherished part of the Byzantine Empire but had recently been taken into independence by Isaac Ducas Comnenus, who claimed to be the island's new governor by producing forged documentation from the centre of the Empire, Constantinople, which would later be known as the city of Istanbul in Turkey. As Cyprus greeted Isaac with open arms, he ditched his Governor title and became, on his own insistence, an

Emperor. He quickly took the island out of the safety of the Byzantine Empire, and forged links with Saladin, the leader of the Muslim Army and the catalyst for Richard's Crusade.

However, it didn't take long for the people of Cyprus to realise their mistake and as Richard's Crusaders came ashore to release Isaac's prisoners the battle for the island began.

The self-styled Emperor publicly announced that whatever rules or treaties Richard proclaimed, they would not bind him. This gave the Crusader King the incentive he needed to mount a full-scale take-over of Cyprus.

On the 12th of May 1191, King Richard and his fiancée, Berengaria, were married at Limassol Castle and immediately afterwards, Richard set about conquering Cyprus. Isaac had hidden himself amongst the castles in the high rugged mountains and left his wife and daughter in the confines of the most inaccessible and easily guarded castle of them all. He surmised that Richard would eventually get bored and move on to the Holy Land, which wasn't a bad plan, but he totally underestimated the tactical genius and quick-thinking of his opponent. Richard simply besieged the castle and captured Isaac's wife and daughter.

Isaac was horrified and gave himself up for surrender on the condition that he should not be clapped in irons. So, Richard had shackles made from silver instead and chained him in those.

Richard The Lionheart and his army continued to join up with King Philip at the siege of Acre. The siege had been running since Saladin and his army captured Jerusalem and ordered the King of Jerusalem, Guy of Lusignan, to never take part in any fighting again. Guy promised to do so until he was out of the city and then found a Priest to break the oath for him, as a Muslim oath was considered breakable for a Christian. Guy then laid siege to the city of Acre, as it was the chief port and the largest town in the Kingdom of Jerusalem. His army grew as the siege continued, but neither side was gaining anything. The stalemate continued for two years, with all Muslim and Christian eyes trained on this small siege.

If Acre fell, it would be the first major blow to their leader, Saladin, who had been so victorious at the Battle of Hattin.

When King Philip of France arrived with his troops, in 1191, he discovered that the only other nobleman there was Duke Leopold of Austria, who had taken charge of the German contingent of the soldiers. Because the Duke was running out of money, all his soldiers defected to the leadership of Philip after he offered them 3 gold pieces. Upon Richard's arrival, a better offer of 4 gold pieces bought the English King command of the troops.

At Acre, both Richard and Philip fell seriously ill with an ailment that is described as an intense fever, which caused their hair and nails to fall out. This didn't stop them bickering with each other over the future spoils of capturing the city, but they eventually agreed on a fifty-fifty split on the spoils of winning the siege. Using wooden catapults, digging at the base of the city's walls to weaken them, and cutting off supplies to the surrounded people, Richard sensed victory and terms of surrender were drawn up. This included the restoration and resurrection of the Holy Cross.

Upon claiming Acre for the Crusaders, the seeds of Richard's downfall were sown when he tore down a banner that Duke Leopold of Austria had put up next to his own and that of King Philip of France.

The planting of the banner implied that Duke Leopold was staking a claim to the loot and showing the world that he too was instrumental in the capture of Acre. Being as this wasn't the case the banner was torn down and the duke was naturally offended. He left Acre within days of the end of the siege and returned to his Austrian homeland, seething with hatred for King Richard of

England.

He was not the only one to feel wronged when both King's took all the bounty for themselves and none of the rewards went to the many Barons and Knights who had been fighting the siege as long, if not longer, as these two greedy Kings. Naturally, even though Philip agreed wholeheartedly with what was happening, it was the strong and blunt King Richard who made the announcements and forced those financially challenged by the siege to return to their homelands, with nothing but the empty cheers of victory ringing in their ears.

After the demands were made to Saladin of a large amount of gold and the release of the prisoners he held, King Philip of France decided to leave Acre and return to rule his country. He had never wanted to be a Crusader in the first place and was more interested in wealth than fame. He promised Richard that he would not attempt to invade any of the English King's territories on his return. This was a promise he found hard to keep.

Saladin could not find the money to hand over to Richard, so the English King allowed him to pay it in instalments. The return of the prisoners from both sides would have boosted morale and secured a lasting truce of peace between two honourable enemies. Unfortunately, with rumours that Saladin had already executed his Christian prisoners, the first instalment was not forthcoming and Richard's set deadline was passed. Acting on King Richard's orders, the lives of the captured Acre garrison were extinguished by the victorious soldiers. They appeared to take great delight in the mass slaughter of two thousand seven hundred captured soldiers, in full view of Saladin's army.

The Christian soldiers saw this brutal and barbaric act of execution as no more than a so-called 'act of God'.

Two days later, King Richard and his army marched out of Acre and on to Jerusalem, their own personal holy grail. On the way there, the mixed nationalities of Richard's Crusading Army suffered waves of attack by Saladin and his army whilst they marched onwards in formation never breaking rank. The rearguard of French Knights took the heaviest beating, as they had to turn to fight, whilst walking backwards, and were never allowed to charge into Saladin's men.

William de Barres fought so nobly during these skirmishes that any grudge that Richard bore him from their lance-tournament in Messina was quickly forgotten and forgiven. King Richard scored many victories after Acre, defeating Saladin at Arsuf, rebuilding Jaffa and Ascalon, and capturing Daron. Richard conquered the entire coast, yet still failed to take the holy city itself.

When they were 12 miles away from Jerusalem, King Richard began to realise that attaining it would be almost impossible. The fact that nobody wanted to stay on and run it, as it was not the 'land of milk and honey' as it had been previously and erroneously described, was also a major factor in his decision to sound the retreat.

In their final encounter at Jaffa, King Richard was outnumbered heavily but he used his considerable skill and knowledge of tactics to defeat Saladin's army of seven thousand with only fifty-four of his own knights and two thousand infantrymen. Saladin held real respect for his worthy adversary, and this was shown after King Richard was unhorsed in battle.

Saladin sent him two fresh horses to continue fighting on and Richard won the day, causing his enemy to retreat to the safety of Jerusalem.

Another major factor for Richard's speedy exit from the Holy Land before taking Jerusalem was the receipt of news about his brother John causing trouble in England and plotting with King Philip of France, who had broken his oath to stay away from Richard's lands. King Richard negotiated a deal with Saladin that there would be a three-year truce between everyone. From Tyre to Jaffa, it would be Christians who ruled. Jerusalem was to be kept by the Muslims, if they allowed Christian pilgrims to visit the city. Saladin agreed and many of Richard's followers took the opportunity to visit Jerusalem.

King Richard decided against doing so himself, only wanting to enter the city as its victor. He had vowed to stay on until the following Easter, but when he heard of the plotting of his brother with the French King, Richard began his long return journey home.

The legendary Saladin, the only man to unite his army against invaders and actually win battles, passed away before Easter of 1193 and, had Richard been there, he would have almost certainly completed his holy quest and taken Jerusalem, unopposed.

King Richard decided to return to England via Germany, by sea. It was a decision that, in hindsight, paved the way for his eventual downfall. He was driven ashore, during a storm, and shipwrecked on German soil. Duke Leopold of Austria managed to capture Richard after hearing of English pilgrims trooping through the countryside.

The English King was imprisoned in a very secure castle, called Durnstein, overlooking the river Danube on a high mountain-slope in lower Austria.

News of Richard's capture reached his younger brother, John, who instantly drew on the Welsh and the Scottish to help him seize control of the English throne with an organised rebellion. Prince John's claim was that he was the rightful heir and that his brother, King Richard, had died in the Crusades.

It was against this backdrop that the legend of Robin Hood emerged to bring hope to the people of England. The heavy burden of taxation imposed by Prince John, as he stood in his brother's place, left the poor starving, while the nobles and barons became richer and richer.

If you travel to Nottingham and Sherwood Forest in England today, you'll find mention of Robin Hood everywhere you go, and although there are numerous versions of the story, the best-loved tale is as follows:

> *Robin of Loxley, a nobleman by birth went off to fight for King Richard in the Crusades. When he returned to his castle and his lands close to Sherwood Forest, they had been taken over by Prince John and his Barons. Robin joined a band of outlaws in Sherwood Forest to fight against Prince John, refusing to believe that King Richard was dead. Because the outlaws wore green-hooded jackets to hide their identities Robin of Loxley soon became known as Robin Hood, and he and his band of merry men stole from the rich to give to the poor. By doing this Robin could undermine Prince John's rule until Richard's return.*

As in all good legends, there is romance in abundance as Robin Hood falls in love with Maid Marian, a beautiful noble lady who is a cousin of King Richard. Despite all manner of trials and tribulations the couple are set to marry in the green wood of Sherwood Forest. It's at this moment that King Richard the Lionheart returns to bless the marriage and take back the throne of England from his brother.

The legend of Robin Hood has certainly been instrumental in painting Richard the Lionheart as a great hero and Prince John, who would be king after his brother, as a black hearted villain. However, in order to find out whether this is fact or fanciful fiction we need to return to what happened next in Richard's story as he languished in his Austrian jail.

Whilst Prince John was claiming the demise of his older brother, King Richard was moved from his imprisonment in Durnstein Castle, Austria, to Speyer, in Germany, to stand trial for the crimes he was alleged to have committed according to Duke Leopold of Austria. During two days in March 1193, Richard pleaded his case and replied to the charges against him so eloquently that instead of blaming him, he was praised and given a kiss of peace by the Emperor of Germany. There was also a promise of an aid to the reconciliation between King Richard of England and King Philip of France.

Nevertheless, Richard's release was wholly dependent upon the sum of one hundred and fifty thousand marks being paid as a ransom, a fee, which included fifty galleys and two hundred Knights a year being supplied for Germany's command. This would explain a sudden rise in English taxation but while the money was being raised, Richard spent his time in good spirits detained in a German castle.

Thanks to Richard's mother Eleanor who had taken charge of keeping her younger son, Prince John, in order, the Crusader King Richard was released and sent back to England once the ransom had been paid. On his return Richard soon discovered the extent of John's mischief, and regaining Nottingham Castle, in the heart of Robin Hood country proved to be something of a battle. Not believing the news of the King's triumphant return, Richard the Lionheart had to lay siege on his own castle to convince them that he was, indeed, their long-lost sovereign. After the initial mistake had been cleared up, Richard spent a day hunting in Sherwood Forest, where folk tales suggest he met and pardoned Robin Hood, possibly at his wedding to Maid Marian.

Most of the castles in John's name immediately switched their allegiance back to their rightful King. Rockingham Castle, in Leicester, was a favourite haunt of John when he sat on the throne, and it is believed that the crown jewels were stored there on one of his last trips North. Rochester Castle in Kent was another of John's preferred castles and even to this day is an imposing fortress for visitors.

After costing England so much in taxes to pay his ransom, the nation deserved a period of stability with Richard attending to the business of state, but the Lionheart evidently had other ideas. It wasn't long before King Richard became an 'absent King' once more as he left for Normandy, to quell King Philip of France's steady march into his overseas domain. The Lionheart would never return to England again. His brother, John, fled from his alliance with King Philip and met up with Richard in Normandy, begging his forgiveness. Richard was benevolent and told him that he was nothing more than an errant child who had been misled, so John was able to return to England and prepare again for more mischief if his brother failed to overthrow King Philip.

Meanwhile, Richard had built a great castle, Chateau Gaillard in northern France to act as a base for operations. He combined his knowledge of siege craft with the strongholds of the East and created the most formidable fortress ever seen. King Philip of France scoffed at his messenger's reports of this gigantic castle and said it would not stay standing for long. Richard, on hearing this comment, replied:

> 'By God's throat!…if yon castle were built of neither iron, nor stone, but wholly of butter, I would without hesitation undertake to hold it securely against him and all his forces.'

This belief in his own invincibility would add to his imminent downfall.

A five-year truce was instigated as Richard stamped his authority on the situation and they began negotiations on the 13th of January 1199.

Such was the animosity between these once great friends that Richard stayed on a boat on the River Seine, whilst Philip sat on horseback on the riverbank. At this point, as our journal is ending it's inevitable on past form that a period of peace would find Richard on the lookout for adventure and sure enough when news reached him of buried treasure at Chalus he was quickly on the trail.

The Lionheart immediately claimed that the treasure was his and set about attacking the little Castle, with its garrison of no more than fifteen poorly armed men. With his usual bravado Richard rode up to the castle's wall in order to find where the weakest point was to attack. Spotted by a lone archer, a crossbow bolt hit him in the left shoulder and enraged him so much that he ordered an all-out attack.

The iron arrowhead proved resistant to removal from the King's shoulder and gangrene soon set in. King Richard knew then that his days were numbered. He wrote to his mother at Fontevraud, expressing a desire for her to be with him at the end of his life, and announced his younger brother, Prince John, as his successor. The archer who fired the arrow that injured Richard was summoned to his deathbed. With all French pride he was unrepentant for his actions, yet the King of England guaranteed his pardon and release. Nevertheless, the archer was detained without Richard's knowledge and executed after Richard had died.

Richard Lionheart gave out at the age of forty one on the 6th of April 1199. He was buried in a tomb in the 12th Century Monastery of Fontevraud Abbey, where his father Henry the Second's body had already been laid to rest.

Five short years later, his mother, Eleanor, was entombed alongside him. She died in her 80s, an incredible age in the 12th Century and Eleanor of Aquitaine has most definitely gone down in history as a woman way ahead of her time.

Richard was succeeded by his brother John, one of the most unpopular English monarchs of them all if urban myth is to be believed. King John was not a man for the people, and he had no great cause to fight for, with the righteous zeal of his brother. Yet ironically his deep love of England meant that he may well have in fact been a better King than Richard ever was, as many of the problems he faced were inherited from his brother's reign and the Lionheart's preoccupation with holy wars and crusades.

In the 21st century there is much that can be learnt from the actions of Richard the Lionheart. It has been said that "Those who cannot remember the past are condemned to repeat it" and even the most cursory glance at the Middle East today proves this to be the case. Way back in Richard's time the belief that a holy war would bring personal salvation and gain entry to the Kingdom of Heaven, whatever atrocities were committed, sounds all too familiar.

The places where Richard and Saladin fought and the bloody battlefields where Muslims and Christians laid down their lives for what they believed in, are the very same locations that are so regularly featured in the global news reports of today and the same issues are still disputed. Sadly, Richard himself died at a relatively young age before he had the opportunity to develop wisdom as a result of his passionate, sometimes barbaric and hot-headed youth. However, with the benefit of hindsight, the modern world has no such excuse.

Richard the Lionheart, King Richard the First of England, was a giant amongst men. He achieved as much as any other King, in terms of wealth, fame, and combat, in a remarkably short space of time, but inevitably at great personal cost. Whether he was a good or bad King is at the end of the day far less important than the legacy his crusades have left behind.

Richard truly possessed the Heart of a Lion, and the echo of its roar can still be heard reverberating around history today, and for those prepared to listen, it is a salutary warning from the past that will forever build a bridge to the future.

THE BRITISH ROYALTY COLLECTION

❖ ❖ ❖

MARY QUEEN OF SCOTS

1553 AD

When you start talking about the Kings and Queens of England, it can get very muddling, and when you throw the Scottish monarchs into the fray as well for good measure, matters tend to get even more complicated! It also does not help that many of the erstwhile sovereigns share names, with a number being the only distinction between them. The confusion is never greater than in the case of Mary Queen of Scots, the subject of our journal, a woman who truly was years ahead of her time.

So, before we begin telling the remarkable story of Mary Queen of Scots, we'll set the scene with a real fast, and sometimes furious race through the history of the Kings and Queens of England, Scotland and even France.

Mary's "Stewart" parents were King James V of Scotland and his French wife, Marie de Guise. At this time neighboring England was ruled by King Henry VIII who was a Tudor. Now, Henry VIII was best known for his six wives, Catherine of Aragon, Anne Boleyn, Jane Seymour, Anne of Cleaves, Katherine Howard and Katherine Parr and if you want to remember what happened to them, there's a little rhyme which goes "divorced, beheaded, died, divorced, beheaded, survived". As a result of all this marital disharmony Henry was excommunicated by the Pope and England broke away from the Catholic faith to become a protestant nation.

Despite his many wives, Henry VIII struggled to produce a male heir and his only legitimate son Edward VI ruled for a very short time. And then the trouble really started. Mary, Henry's daughter from his marriage to Catherine of Aragon, succeeded to the throne in the absence of any suitable males. Brought up as a devout Catholic, Mary restored England's links with Rome, and her viscous persecution of Protestants resulted in her earning the title "Bloody Mary".

However, she did not last long either and was succeeded by Henry's daughter by Anne Boleyn, Elizabeth I, who also happened to be the cousin of Mary Queen of Scots. As Henry had broken with Rome to marry Elizabeth's mother, the new Queen was a Protestant and when she came to power, she restored the Protestant Church of England. These were dangerous times, and many people lost their lives simply for being of the wrong faith during the reigns of these two half-sisters.

As complicated as all this sounds it really will help, because after the death of James V of Scotland, our Mary, was crowned Queen of Scotland when she was just nine months old. Later as the story develops, we end up with Elizabeth I, as a Protestant on the throne of England, and her cousin Mary, as a devout Catholic on the throne of Scotland. This would dominate the lives of both women and ultimately result in tragedy for one of them. But we are getting ahead of ourselves in our search to find the woman behind the legend that is Mary Queen of Scots.

There is a delightful old nursery rhyme that children still say to this day, all over Great Britain, and many people believe it is about Mary Queen of Scots, suggesting that down through the ages her story has been a source of immense fascination.

> "Mary, Mary, quite contrary,
> How does your garden grow?
> With silver bells and cockleshells
> And pretty maids all in a row."

The first line – *'Mary, Mary, Quite Contrary'* – is a reference to the fact that she was a ruling Queen rather than a King, because she should not have been ruling at all, according to a 14th Century law that decreed the Scottish Crown should only be inherited by men, unless the male line had become extinct. Which is precisely what happened when King James V died, something he realised just before his tragic end, when Mary was born.

'*Woe is me! My dynasty came with a lass. It will pass with a lass*'.

A "lass" is a Scottish term for a girl or woman, and actually the Stewart dynasty he was speaking of, began with the daughter of that much better-known Scottish King, Robert the Bruce.

The '*How does your garden grow*' part of the rhyme refers to Mary ruling over the vast landscape of Scotland, with its magnificent rolling hills and windswept, rain-soaked valleys that have inspired so many poets, artists, and writers. '*With silver bells and cockleshells*' refers to the fact that she was a devout Roman Catholic. Silver bells are used in Catholic services and the 'cockle shell' is the symbol used for the shrine of Saint James, significant to those of the Catholic Faith.

The '*Pretty maids all in a row*' are thought to be a reference to the execution of Mary Queen of Scots, as a 'maid' was an early device that pre-dated the French guillotine, used for severing heads. However, it is more likely that this line actually refers to her four closest friends, all called Mary, the daughters of Scottish nobility, who were her constant companions.

But then again, you were warned that things could get very confusing, as many people believe that this rhyme is about Queen Mary of England, Elizabeth the First's older sister, with a much more unpleasant translation that we will not elaborate on. So, you can see for yourself how Mary Stuart of Scotland and Mary Tudor of England can be easily muddled. Let us put the record straight.

Mary's "Stewart" parents were King James V of Scotland and his French wife, Marie de Guise. At this time neighboring England was ruled by King Henry VIII who was a Tudor.

Mary Stuart, the future Queen of the Scots, was born on 8th December 1542, at Linlithgow Palance, fifteen miles to the west of Scotland's capital, Edinburgh. This majestic palace was an important landmark for the Stuart dynasty, and Mary returned to the Palace many times during her reign. The Palace itself is something of a hollow shell today, having been damaged by fire in 1746, but restored and renovated by Historic Scotland.

However, the grand towering walls of the outer and inner circle, along with several of the once grand apartments remain standing, almost perfectly intact, making Linlithgow an impressive place to visit on any Scottish tour. In fact, many weddings are celebrated there today, in these truly magnificent surroundings. But there was little joy at Mary's birth back in 1542 as a month before her arrival, her father, King James V, had been defeated by the English in a disastrous battle at Solway Moss that left him broken and depressed.

With Royal dynasties all being connected, it won't come as any surprise that James V of Scotland was the nephew of Henry VIII of England, and he bitterly opposed his uncle's break from the Catholic faith, and he refused to even speak to Henry. This infuriated the King of England, and he began sending legions of troops to re-claim Scotland and take away Scottish Independence as a punishment.

The biggest of the battles took place at Solway Moss, a large marshy peat bog just to the south of the Scottish borders in the English county of Cumbria, which resulted in up to 20,000 Scottish soldiers being overpowered by a much smaller English army of as little as 3,000 men. This was a truly humiliating defeat for the King of Scotland, who hadn't been present at the battle because he'd been forced to retreat to Falkland Palace with a high fever that had developed from a common cold. Falkland Palace was the pride and joy of King James V, who had added extensively to this Royal residence, transforming it into a sophisticated Renaissance Palace of real beauty.

It was James who was responsible for adding such luxuries as a royal tennis court to Falkland Palace, which still survives to this day. However, he had little opportunity to enjoy his handiwork as just two weeks after the battle of Solway Moss, the young King, barely thirty years old, died as a result of the complications from his head cold on December 14th, 1542. His daughter Mary was just seven days old.

This was the second time that the unfortunate Marie de Guise had been widowed in the space of eight years.

Her first marriage had been to the Duke of Longueville in the palace of the Louvres in Paris, and ironically the couple had travelled to Scotland to attend the wedding of King James the Fifth and Princess Madeleine of France. Within a few weeks of marrying, Princess Madeleine who was suffering from tuberculosis succumbed to the cold and wet Scottish climate and died. Then a few years later, Marie's husband the duke also died and James V of Scotland who needed an alliance with France against his uncle, King Henry VIII asked for her hand. It is interesting to note that Henry had also shown an interest in the 21-year-old widowed Marie, as he was himself between wives, and she had given the duke two healthy sons, and Henry craved a male heir above all things.

Marie chose the Scottish throne and was crowned Queen of Scotland at Edinburgh Castle in 1540. She was an instant success with her adopted people as the first thing she did was to learn the language, and then she promptly produced an heir to the Scottish throne, called James.

However, King James, the baby's father, was becoming increasingly prone to paranoid bouts of depression, believing that the nobility of Scotland was plotting with England against him. He even executed several of his closest friends with no evidence whatsoever. Marie then gave birth to a second son, Robert, in 1541, but within days of the christening, both he and his elder brother James were dead. The circumstances were suspicious to say the least, and it is alleged that the family of one the nobles the King had executed was responsible for poisoning the little boys. If you travel to Edinburgh and visit the magnificent Holyrood Palace, the two Princes were buried in the peaceful surroundings of Holyrood Abbey.

Although it is now little more than a ruin, due to an 18th Century roof collapse, the building still has a majestic quality next to the imposing Palace that is to this day the official Scottish residence of the reigning monarch, Queen Elizabeth II. If Holyrood sounds a strange word, 'Rood' is an old Scottish term for a 'cross', so the Palace and the Abbey literally translate as Holy Cross.

Traumatic as all this must have been for the King and Queen, the state of the Scottish nation was also deeply disturbed. Scheming and plotting were going on everywhere and due to malicious rumours, James and Marie grew further and further apart. She was accused of adulterous affairs, and he took up with a string of mistresses, fathering several illegitimate offspring.

Somehow amidst all this turmoil Marie became pregnant again, this time with a girl, the Mary of our story, and as we already know, within days of the birth, her father, James V, King of Scotland died, leaving the tiny baby girl as the only rightful heir to the Scottish throne.

After what had happened to her little boys, Queen Marie was justifiably afraid for her daughter and faced a tough decision, either return to France and relative safety, or stay in Scotland as Queen Regent.

To leave Scotland would have meant leaving baby Mary behind, which was unthinkable, so Queen Marie decided to stay and do everything possible to stabilise the situation.

The little girl was just nine months old when she was crowned Mary Queen of Scots, in the Chapel Royal at Stirling Castle, Scotland, on December 9th 1543. This unique ceremony saw Mary dressed in heavy regal robes that had been specially created in miniature. She even had a train of ermine, a jewelled satin gown, huge, long sleeves, and a velvet mantle. She was sat *in* the throne of Scotland but had to be held upright by the presiding Lord Chancellor.

While all this was going on, King Henry VIII still had his eye on Scotland, and he decided that Mary Queen of Scots should be married to his son Edward to unite England and Scotland as one nation. To achieve this, he set out to dominate Scotland and this was known as the Rough Wooing, and indeed it was. Queen Marie, the child's mother was forbidden to leave Stirling Castle, a huge fortress perched on a hilltop with high cliffs to three sides, leaving her unable to contact her family in France for help.

Then King Henry VIII died suddenly in January 1547, and he was succeeded by little Mary's child fiancé Edward. The English throne was controlled by the Earl of Hertford as Edward wasn't of age, and he swiftly invaded Scotland to claim it as part of England. To cement this alliance Hertford was determined to force through the marriage that Henry VIII had arranged between the child monarchs.

However, he had not counted on the determination of Mary's mother who begged for help from France. Assistance came in the form of a marriage proposal from the King no less, requesting Mary's hand for his new-born son, the Dauphin Francois. The Dauphin was the term used for the heir to the French throne, while if he had a wife, she was known as the Dauphine. Queen Marie agreed, and with the blessing of the Scottish Parliament sent her daughter to the French Court.

By all accounts Mary was a delightful child, graceful, pretty, and intelligent. The French people took her to their hearts and the King himself no less described her as the most perfect child he had ever seen.

Mary's travelling companions were the 'Four Marys', Mary Fleming, Mary Seton, Mary Beaton, and Mary Livingstone all of whom were the daughters of Scottish noblemen. They would remain with their namesake for her whole life, right through from her marriage to the Dauphin to her arrest, imprisonment, and eventual execution some forty years later.

According to sources close to the Royal Family, when the Dauphin met Mary for the first time, they were immediately friendly and affectionate towards each other. He was four years old, whilst Mary was a year older. These were peaceful years in France, after the turmoil of the Scottish court and Mary was educated in the traditional manner of a French Princess. She was taught how to speak French, Latin, Italian, Spanish and Greek, she learned to sing and dance, and also how to play musical instruments. Mary was tutored in religious matters by a Scottish priest and in 1558, she married the Dauphin of France in Notre-Dame Cathedral, Paris.

In all Mary enjoyed thirteen good years in France and her marriage was evidently happy, but as we all know thirteen is considered unlucky, and in the case of the young Queen of France and Scotland the fates were most definitely set against her. Within the space of a year, her mother, who had been keeping the peace in Scotland died, and even more tragically so did Mary's husband, shortly after being crowned King of France.

There was no other option for the eighteen-year-old widow; Mary was Queen of Scotland, and she needed to take control of her birthright. Her destination was Edinburgh and she arrived at the great city's port of Leith. In honour of her French heritage,

Mary Stuart changed the spelling of her surname from the Scottish way – S.T.E.W.A.R.T. – to the French version – S.T.U.A.R.T. – and therefore you will find two spellings of the Stuart name in the history books, before and after, Mary's arrival in Scotland in 1561.

Without her husband or her mother, Mary may well have considered looking to England for comfort, where her cousin Elizabeth had been Queen since 1558. However, Elizabeth had already developed a deep distrust of Mary, through circumstances beyond the Scottish Queen's control. When Elizabeth was crowned, the Catholics believed she had no right to rule, and urged Mary to step forward as the only legitimate and Catholic heir to the throne of England. It was the start of a troubled relationship between the two women that would without doubt damage them both.

So, Mary followed her own course, taking her rightful place as Queen of Scotland, vowing that she would continue in her mother's footsteps, and keep the peace between the feuding Scottish noble lords.

Also, religious differences were causing all sorts of problems in Scotland as well. Just a year before Mary's arrival, the Scottish Reformation, led by the fiery preacher John Knox, declared Scotland protestant. As Mary herself was a devout Catholic she advocated a policy of religious tolerance, but John Knox was not inclined to return the favour.

In general Queen Mary seemed to be getting by with little need for strong-arm tactics, while her gentle approach and charming French manners helped the people warm to her, with one notable exception. John Knox!

At the time of Queen Mary's return, he was Edinburgh's most powerful minister, based at Edinburgh's magnificent St Giles Cathedral, an awe-inspiring gothic edifice, from where he used to rant and rave in his sermons about the frivolity and heresy of the Scottish Queen. Remember she was young, attractive, and used to being flattered and adored, but the pious clergyman was having none of it.

Knox published pamphlets, like the *'First Blast of The Trumpet Against the Monstrous Regiment of Women'*, in which he attacked and argued against a female monarch, writing that female rulers were most odious in the presence of God and were undeniably traitors and rebels against the almighty.

John Knox certainly proved to be a thorn in Mary's flesh, and to this day you can still visit his imposing house, now a museum, on Edinburgh's Royal Mile, not far from where he presided over the pulpit in St Giles Cathedral.

Incidentally, the Royal Mile is the name of the road that joins the magnificent fortress that is Edinburgh Castle with the grandeur of Holyrood Palace, and Mary Queen of Scots would come to know both Royal houses very well indeed, in the first instance making her home at Holyrood. In fact, it was in this very Palace that Mary quite suddenly, and some would say inexplicably, married her first cousin, Henry Stewart, Lord Darnley. At first the people of Scotland were shocked by their Queen's rash behaviour, but Mary knew they would quickly get used to the idea, especially if she could produce a son and heir for the nation. Despite her efforts since arriving, the Scottish Lords had continually battled against each other, but a Stuart Prince would keep the Scottish crown safe, whatever happened.

In retrospect, it's hard to imagine why Mary chose to marry Darnley, an immature, unpopular nineteen-year-old, who was known to have a particularly unpleasant violent streak. But perhaps she simply made the best of a bad lot. At least Darnley had Royal blood and could be controlled, or so Mary might have thought, as he was only crowned King Consort, which essentially meant he had the title of King but none of the powers.

Darnley was eager to make such an advantageous match hoping to eventually rule England as well as Scotland, as it was likely that if Elizabeth I did not marry and have children of her own, Mary would by default become the English Queen's heir.

But Mary was disappointed with her choice very early in the marriage. No doubt Darnley was charming while he was wooing her, but after the marriage vows had been exchanged it was a different story. Spoiled, petulant, and given to mood swings, Darnley became a pawn for the Scottish nobles who were just waiting for an opportunity to remove Mary from power.

Matters deteriorated further, ironically when Mary did become pregnant, as Darnley perhaps realised that a son would become King of a unified Scotland and England rather than him. A tragic turn of events occurred at Holyrood when Mary was forced to witness the brutal murder of her private secretary and great friend, David Rizzio. The Queen was five months pregnant at the time and one school of thought is that Darnley, who was involved in the horrific killing, was hoping to cause his wife to miscarry. However, others believe that Rizzio was Mary's lover and the child she was carrying was in fact his rather than Darnley's, making revenge the motive rather than anything more sinister.

If Mary had thought her life troubled before, she now found herself pregnant with a violent husband begging her forgiveness and coping with the loss of her dearest friend at the Scottish court. As Queen she granted Darnley a pardon, but their relationship had been destroyed.

John Knox, the Protestant preacher who had spent the seven years of Mary's reign verbally attacking her at every opportunity from the pulpit of St Giles Cathedral, openly praised the murder of David Rizzio.

Knox believed the worst of Mary, and with public opinion split as well as her husband's treachery, she knew she would have to take steps to protect her unborn child. With great care she managed to smuggle a message out of the Palace to a loyal Scottish Lord

called James Hepburn, Duke of Orkney, and the 4th Earl of Bothwell, who took the distraught Queen to Edinburgh Castle and comparative safety.

Three months and ten days later, on the 19$^{th\ of}$ June 1566, Mary's son James was born after a long and painful labour, the rightful heir to the Scottish throne. He was baptized a Catholic in the Chapel of Stirling Castle a short distance from Edinburgh, much to the disgust of both the preacher John Knox and Queen Elizabeth I. At 23 years of age Mary had provided Scotland with a rightful heir to the Stuart dynasty; she now held power over the feuding Scottish Lords because of her son, but in personal terms her own life lay in ruins.

Mary turned to Bothwell, who had protected her in the past as a valued personal advisor, as Darnley became sidelined and despised by the Scottish nobles, who now supported Mary. In fear of his own life, Darnley, ever the coward, decided to escape to France. He got as far as the city of Glasgow, still in Scotland, and had to rest there because of illness. Medical reports at the time suggest that this may have been syphilis, contracted before he married Mary. The fact that he didn't pass this disease on to his wife is often cited as another indication that Mary's son, James VI of Scotland was not his son.

Nevertheless, Mary did her duty as a wife and attended her husband on his sickbed in Glasgow, allowing him to rest and recover before returning with him to Edinburgh Castle, and surprisingly reconciliation was even considered.

Then Darnley decided at the last minute to stay elsewhere rather than risk infecting his son. The house was at Kirk O'Field not far from Edinburgh, but Mary chose not to remain with him. On

February 13th, 1563, unluckily for Darnley, a huge explosion tore through the house and was even felt on the streets of Edinburgh. Gunpowder had filled the chamber bellow Darnley's rooms and the finger of suspicion immediately pointed in Bothwell's direction. Ironically, when Darnley's body was found the only marks upon it were of strangulation and it's believed he realised what was happening and tried to escape. The fact that he'd been strangled implies he was prevented from doing this, and the plot curiously thickens.

It doesn't take much detective work to add two and two together to get five. Did Mary really attempt reconciliation with Darnley, or was she, under Bothwell's instruction luring him into a trap? It was all too coincidental for the canny Scots who became very suspicious of the Queen's part in the murder and more importantly Bothwell's influence over her.

What happened next in this strange saga relies a great deal on conjecture as Mary went to visit her son James at Sterling Castle. It would be the last meeting of mother and child as the series of events that followed sealed Mary's tragic fate.

On her return from Sterling to Edinburgh Mary was kidnapped by Bothwell, although some accounts suggest that she was a more than willing captive. The next thing that the people of Scotland knew was that in the May of 1567, Queen Mary married the Earl of Bothwell at the Palace of Holyrood. They were not best pleased, and John Knox demanded that the pair be brought to justice for Darnley's murder.

A mere month into the Royal marriage, the Scottish Lords decided that Bothwell was a dangerous man to hold so much power and was a considerably worse prospect as the Queen's husband than even Darnley had been. The battle lines were quickly drawn, and Mary realised that her marriage had compromised her position, so in order to avoid bloodshed, when an army of rebel nobles and their forces met her own troops at Carberry Hill, eight miles south-east of Edinburgh, she handed herself over to them as a prisoner.

Mary Queen of Scots was then taken to yet another Scottish castle, this time Lochleven, a small square fortress on an island in the middle of a Loch, strategically placed between the towns of Edinburgh, Stirling and Perth. Today this is a truly beautiful place, cared for by Historic Scotland and it's hard to imagine a more romantic location, but for Mary there would be little to cheer her within its walls, as Lochleven was just another in a series of castle prisons in which she would spend the rest of her days.

However, in the 16th Century, Lochleven Castle was much bigger than its ruins would suggest, and it certainly had a distinguished list of previous occupants.

William Wallace, the famous Scottish rebel better known since Mel Gibson's movie as Braveheart, stormed the castle to win it back from the English, who had violated Scotland and her people so brutally.

Getting back to Mary Queen of Scot's enforced stay at Lochleven there is another great mystery that surrounds this unfortunate young woman. Whilst a captive in the care of the castle's owner, Sir William Douglas, she is believed to have given birth to twins, fathered by either Darnley or Bothwell. Many believe that the infants were stillborn, while others romanticise about them being smuggled off the island and whisked away to the safety of France, as people search for some kind of happy ending to this tragic tale.

On the 24th of July 1567, in a weakened state from the difficult birth of the mysterious twins, Mary was forced to sign abdication papers sent by the Scottish Lords to give up her claim to the Scottish throne allowing her one-year old son, James, be crowned in her place as King James the Sixth of Scotland. Left in peace after her acquiescence Mary's health began to improve and she immediately started to plot her escape from Lochleven Castle. First, she sent pleading letters of help to her cousin Queen Elizabeth in England, who totally ignored Mary's plight.

With no option available, Mary escaped her castle prison on May 2nd, 1568, with the help of the youngest son of Sir Willliam Douglas, who smuggled Mary, dressed as a servant girl, across the loch in a rowing boat to a group of waiting Scottish Lords who were sympathetic to the Stuart cause.

Together, they raised an army of 600 men but were soon defeated when they went into battle. Mary then made the unprecedented decision to journey south to England, in order to ask for the support of Queen Elizabeth the First, who had avoided many of the difficulties that Mary had faced by never marrying.

Unfortunately help was once again not forthcoming. Queen Elizabeth had several options she could legitimately take, one being to send Mary back to the Sottish nobles, which would've been a cruel fate for a woman who had done her no harm. Alternatively, she could exile the Scottish Queen to France, which would probably have been the kindest option for Mary but could well have compromised Elizabeth's position. Mary would have been a powerful pawn in the hands of the French King to use against the English throne.

Then again Elizabeth could forcibly restore Mary to her position as Queen of Scotland, but that would cause conflict between the two nations all over again. Eventually she chose to imprison Mary in England, although this was dangerous because the Catholic Queen would be perceived by Elizabeth's enemies as a figure head for any plots to overthrow the protestant pretender.

To avoid this happening, Elizabeth kept moving Mary from Castle to Castle as her political prisoner. Catholic Plots grew thick and fast and always Mary's name was attached to them, somewhere in the background. Elizabeth's paranoia increased as the years passed by and Mary lived out her days with only a handful of loyal companions by her side and she would probably have known nothing of the plots bearing her name.

Eventually Elizabeth bowed to the pressure of her advisers who wanted the threat posed by Mary eliminated and the Queen of Scots was put on trial for the murder of Darnley.

This trial took place without Mary present, so she was unable to defend herself, and revolved around a series of letters and documents written to Bothwell before they were married. These love letters and poems were the only evidence against her, and they were probably forgeries created to imply Mary was an unfit mother and adulteress. They were called the Casket Letters, as

they had been kept in a silver casket, and even by 16th Century legal standards could not have proved Mary guilty of anything! However, the court delivered a guilty verdict, and everyone waited to see what Elizabeth would do next.

The Queen of England did nothing, and Mary continued her existence within the walls of her castle prisons. Bothwell had fled Scotland and sought refuge in Denmark where eventually his life of drink and debauchery caught up with him. An angry father whose daughter had been taken advantage of by Bothwell locked him up in a Copenhagen Castle, chained to a dungeon wall with a low roof that didn't allow him to stand up straight. The King of Denmark thought a ransom could be extracted for the Scottish nobleman, but nobody wanted to pay. After all his scheming and plotting Bothwell died insane and alone in a strange land, his dreams of ruling Scotland and England never fulfilled.

Elizabeth I was a difficult woman to manipulate and those who thought Mary's trial over the Casket Letters would result in the Queen of Scot's execution were disappointed.

The Queen of England stubbornly continued her policy of moving Mary from Castle to Castle for 19 long years, in which time her son, James the Sixth of Scotland, had reached his fifteenth birthday and assumed the throne of Scotland outright. He had been raised a Protestant by his kidnappers and, because of this, did nothing to help his mother imprisoned in England, in fact he had no communication with her whatsoever.

Catholic sympathisers came and went, plots on the protestant Queen's life were foiled but Elizabeth never let Mary stand trial again for another eighteen years. However, the persecution of Catholics increased and a visit to Harvington Hall, a fine house of the period that belonged to a family that secretly kept faith with Rome, illustrates just how serious a business this really was. In almost every room are concealed Priest holes were the men who travelled the country to say Mass with the faithful could be hidden. The penalty for this act of worship was death, for the Catholic priest and the household, and the Priest holes saved many lives. But it was an issue that continued to threaten Elizabeth's position, on a personal and political level and eventually a law was passed that deemed any Catholic plot against the Queen of England, regardless of whether it was instigated by Mary or not, would result in the Queen of Scots being tried for treason.

Sir Francis Walsingham, England's Secretary of State was responsible for Elizabeth's safety, and he was certainly keen to remove the problem of Mary Queen of Scots once and for all. A plan was hatched and cleverly executed that has gone down in history as the Babington Plot, consisting of secret letters between Mary and Sir Anthony Babington.

Walsingham had the letters added to with a forged postscript and Mary's fate was sealed, she was implicated in a conspiracy to assassinate Elizabeth. Mary, Queen of Scots was moved to Fotheringhay Castle, in September 1586, to stand trial for treason. Despite strenuously denying the accusation with a spirited defence, she was found guilty. One of her more memorable comments during her trial was

> "Remember Gentlemen the Theatre of history is wider than the Realm of England!"

Fotheringhay Castle stood in Northamptonshire, about 12 miles west of Peterborough, and there is little left to see today apart from a few stones and a grass covered mound. But for Mary it was yet another castle prison, however this time, unbeknown to her, it was to be her last. She wasn't told the outcome of her trial and it was months later, on the 7th of February 1587, that Mary learned she was to be executed the next day.

Rumour has it that Queen Elizabeth still hadn't wanted to see her cousin beheaded and only signed the death warrant in error believing the document to be something else. But whatever the truth, Walsingham and his supporters had what they'd wanted for a very long time and on this occasion, there was no reprieve for the ill-fated Queen of Scotland.

Mary entered the Great Hall at Fotheringhay Castle on the 8th of February 1587, knowing that unlike the 200 or more spectators, she would never leave again. She wore black satin and velvet, but as she reached the block, the outer garments were cast off to reveal a dress of red, the colour of Catholic martyrdom.

It's reported that it took four attempts for the executioner to fulfil his task and after the first blow failed, Mary is said to have cried out 'Sweet Jesus!' This must have been a horrific enough spectacle, but worse was to come, as the Scottish Queen's headless body began to move. Mary's faithful pet dog, a little Terrier called Skye, had been hiding under the red skirt, and had been present throughout the entire brutal affair.

However, the suffering was at last at an end, and although Mary would have undoubtedly preferred a swifter departure from this world, her prayer on the day of her death suggests that the twenty years she had spent in captivity never knowing which day was to be her last had taken its toll!

> *O my Lord and my God, I have trusted in thee.*
> *O my dear Jesus, now liberate me.*
> *In shackle and chain, in torture and pain, I long for thee.*
> *In weakness and sighing, kneeling and crying,*
> *I adore and implore thee to liberate me.*

This was a poignant end for the once light-hearted, fun loving, elegant, witty, tolerant, and beautiful Mary Queen of Scots who had spent her whole life being a political pawn by virtue of her birth. Some would say it was her terrible choice in men that was her down fall, others that her pretty face had been the real reason for her cousin Queen Elizabeth turning against her, but this is indeed always going to be a story open to speculation.

However, the one thing that we do know for sure is that out of this turmoil, James VI of Scotland, Mary's son, united the two nations when he was crowned James I of England after Queen Elizabeth's death in 1603.

It's highly probable, if contemporary records are to be believed, that King James I wasn't a particular nice man to know, but all agree that he was a remarkable monarch, writing a new page in the history books, ruling over the first United Kingdom.

Eventually, (it took until 1612), James moved the body of his mother Mary, from a simple tomb in Peterborough Cathedral, close to Fotheringhay, to a magnificent tomb in Westminster Abbey, as befitted the once Queen of Scotland and France.

Ironically the three most powerful women of the Tudor and

Stuart dynasties lie in state very close to each other in Westminster Abbey. Queen Mary I of England, better known to us now as Bloody Mary is buried with her sister Queen Elizabeth I, and the Latin inscription translates as:

"Partners both in throne and grave, here rest we two sisters, Elizabeth and Mary in the hope of one resurrection".

An appropriate postscript would be "and Cousin Mary too" because the tomb of Mary Queen of Scots lies just about 9meters away, but few who pass this way will ever appreciate the irony.

Whatever their struggle in life, monarchy, religion and in Mary Queen of Scot's case, men, these three women, who had more in common than they ever got the opportunity to realise, in a different set of circumstances might well have been the greatest of friends.

LIAM DALE

ROYAL ROMANCES - THE BRITISH MONARCHY

When you look back in history at royal romances, surprising as it may seem, few have happy ever after endings, and in many instances the idea of "Love and Marriage" being inextricably linked is not quite as common as you might at first think. In fairy stories handsome Kings and Princes regularly sweep fair maidens off their feet, transforming them into Princesses and Queens, and although a rarer occurrence, a Royal Princess can create a Prince out of the most unpromising of characters!

But in real life, as most of us know, the course of true love never runs smoothly, and in the case of so many highly publicized "Royal Romances", past and present, the pursuit of love can be even more hazardous!

The main reason for this is the significance of the Royal Romance when it comes to the line of succession, as every Royal Dynasty down through the ages has relied upon a healthy supply of legitimate heirs to consolidate its right to rule. The pressure this has put upon monarchs and monarchs-in-waiting to marry the most suitable Princes or Princesses isn't always a recipe for wedded bliss, although there have been occasions when prospective brides and grooms met each other for the first time on the way to the Royal Chapel, and went on to enjoy a long, happy, fulfilling, fruitful and faithful alliance.

Now, should you be thinking that this all sounds very contrived and calculating, as images of the chivalrous King Arthur in full knightly attire, astride a galloping white charger in search of Queen Guinevere spring to mind, you do sometimes have to delve a little deeper. And when it comes to romance, things aren't always as straightforward as history might at first glance suggest.

Travelling around Great Britain there are any number of locations that claim to relate to the legendary King, from the mountains and valleys of Wales, over the mystical Bodmin Moor to the wild Cornish coast at Tintagel and Land's End. But if you're looking for Camelot, King Arthur's legendary court, where he presided over his magnificent Round Table, your journey could well bring you to the Roman fort at Caerleon in Gwent on one day and take you to the Great Hall at Winchester the next! And to confuse matters still further, the graves of Arthur and Guinevere can be found amongst the ruins at Glastonbury Abbey, or so the legend goes.

The story of Arthur and Guinevere is still the foundation for many books and films, with each new generation that discovers this all-time great romance, telling their own version of Royal love and loss.

Upon realizing that King Arthur's most influential advisor was a magician called Merlin, it's evident that this is perhaps not the most fact based of romances, but when the successful, older King spotted the beautiful young Guinevere, he asked Merlin to make all the arrangements for a Royal marriage, with the girl's father.

Merlin was reluctant to do so, as he could see into the future and believed any union between the pair was doomed. Even so when pressed by the love-struck Arthur further, against his better judgement, Merlin arranged the marriage, which was celebrated the length and breadth of the land. And one wedding gift was so well received, it's gone down in history, namely a certain Round Table, given by the father of the bride, where Arthur's Knights would all be given their place.

All was well until one of these Knights, Sir Lancelot, fell in love with the Queen, who was quite literally swept of her feet by this Knight in shining armour. Merlin's words of warning proved to be well founded and King Arthur's Camelot was shattered. Arthur was killed in battle, by one of his other Knights, Sir Mordred and legend has it that he sleeps beneath Cadbury Castle in Somerset, ready to return to save the nation if it's ever in danger again. In fact, whatever their differences in life, it's said that all of Arthur's Knights are also sleeping here in case their services are ever needed. Interestingly this hill is just a short distance from Glastonbury, making the graves amongst the Abbey ruins rather redundant; nothing more than a good story promoted by the monks to bring them pilgrims and prosperity.

Placing all this historically is rather tricky, as any evidence of a King Arthur belongs to the 5th Century AD, just after the Romans, left Britain, but the popular image we all have of Arthur and his Queen is far more in keeping with the 12th Century.

This is because a Welsh Bishop, known as Geoffrey of Monmouth in honor of the lovely border town where he originated, wrote the "History of the Kings of Britain" during the early 1100s, and where factual evidence was missing, he allowed his imagination to re-create the story.

This just goes to show how careful we need to be with "history", and when it comes to romance there are many Royal tales told that have been subject to fanciful interpretation over the years. So, after the classic love story of Arthur and Guinevere, we'll move on to a more accurately recorded era, well at least for the times and places of births, marriages and deaths, if not for the more secret matters of the heart.

While Geoffrey of Monmouth was busy writing about the Kings

of Britain's past, in the 12th Century, the Royal family of his time were equally as fascinating as any of the stories he had to tell. For most people Richard Ist, the Lionheart, is the best-known King of this century. With his connections to the Robin Hood story, there is a great deal of romance surrounding him, but his own marriage to Berengaria of Navarre *(Navair)* was far from successful, in part due to his constant absences away on the Crusades.

It's been suggested though that this was not the reason for the lack of offspring, as some think that it was his wife's brother, Sancho, who was the real object of his affection, and the Royal marriage was never actually consummated.

It's therefore fair to say that Richard 1st is perhaps not the best of Kings to feature in this journal, despite early indications to the contrary, and it is in fact Richard's father, Henry the 2nd, who has more to offer the true romantic in search of a King who knew how to woo the ladies.

Even as a young man Henry of Anjou was a handsome hero and a force to be reckoned with. His mother Matilda had been promised the throne of England after the death of her father Henry Ist, who made the Barons promise to accept her as his heir. When he died, they reneged on the deal, and the crown passed to his nephew Stephen. This resulted in years of Civil War, that was only resolved when young Henry raised an army and King Stephen agreed to name Matilda's son as his heir.

Stephen died in 1154 and when Henry was crowned King at Westminster Abbey, the handsome French born twenty-one-year-old brought with him a Queen, his French wife, Eleanor of Aquitaine. It was an interesting match, with the bride being about eleven years older than the groom, and she had previously been married to the French sovereign Louis the 7th. Eleanor claimed she had thought to marry a King only to find she'd married a monk, and the charismatic, passionate, well-educated woman who had also been the most eligible heiress in all of France, sought an annulment from the Pope, which was granted on the grounds of consanguinity that basically means they were too closely related.

Ironically, she was even more closely related to Henry, her second husband, and if rumors are to be believed she had an affair with his father before him, which resulted in Geoffrey of Anjou advising his son against marrying his chosen bride.

It's possible that the chemistry between Eleanor and Henry was electric in the early days, but overall, the marriage was as stormy as both of their personalities.

That Henry was unfaithful to his Queen is undisputed and his choice of mistresses was varied to say the least. The mother of his illegitimate son, Geoffrey, who went on to become Archbishop of York, was described by a medieval writer at Henry the 2nd's court as being, a "base-born, common harlot who stooped to all uncleanliness". Henry also fathered illegitimate children with Alys of France, the daughter of Eleanor's former husband, Louis the 7th and his second wife Constance of Castile, and if that wasn't complicated enough, Henry was supposed to look after her, as she was betrothed to his son Richard the Lionheart, of Robin Hood fame, mentioned earlier.

Over a period of thirteen years Eleanor provided Henry with five sons and three daughters, but by the time the last child, John was born, the marriage was in effect over. Again, this hardly sounds like a first-rate romance, but one of the major factors in the deterioration of Eleanor and Henry's marriage was a lady who we know very little about, generally referred to as "The Fair Rosamund", who the King was quite openly head over heels in love with.

To discover more, we need to travel to the beautiful Gloucestershire countryside where England meets Wales. The border regions known as the Welsh Marches were controlled by the "Marcher" Lords, often of Norman descent, with strong ties to the English Kings and Henry the 2nd met his "Fair Rosamund" while visiting her father, a "Marcher" Lord.

The wonderful Manor House, Flaxley Abbey, founded in 1148, a former Cistercian Abbey in the Forest of Dean, was built on land granted by Henry the 2nd and while records exist of later monarchs staying at the Abbey while hunting in the Royal Forest, there's been speculation that Henry and Rosamund might have met in secret here, when the King was in the district.

Nevertheless, this Royal love story is most frequently associated with Woodstock in Oxfordshire, where the magnificent Blenheim Palace stands today. Long before the classical architecture of Vanbrugh dominated the scene, Henry installed Rosamund in a lodge here. Legend has it that Eleanor discovered what became known as "Fair Rosamund's Bower", and the jealous Queen is alleged to have poisoned her rival, who died in 1176.

Although a good story, this is unlikely to be true, as Eleanor was spending more time away from Henry, attending to her lands in France, with the Royal couple having all but separated. As time passed, she took revenge on her philandering husband by turning his sons, especially her favorite, Richard, against him, which eventually led to Henry's downfall and death at the age of 56.

It has been reported that when Henry had no choice but to make peace with his son Richard, he secretly whispered "May the Lord never permit me to die until I have taken due vengeance upon you". The Queen of Aquitaine had over time proved to be more than a match for her unfaithful husband, and as she outlived both Henry the 2nd and their son Richard I, dying at the incredible age of 82, her influence as the Dowager Queen continue into the 13th Centuy, making Eleanor a veritable tigress to her son's Lionheart.

Down through the ages, it is unusual to find a Queen with the wealth, power, survival skills and sheer manipulative cunning of Eleanor of Aquitaine, and as we move on three hundred years to the time of King Henry the Eighth, you can't help wondering if this much married monarch had found himself with a wife of Eleanor's metal, history might have had a very different outcome.

When Richard the 3rd of the Royal House of York famously cried "A horse, a horse, a Kingdom for a horse" in the version of events dramatized by the Great Bard of Avon William Shakespeare, he was engaged in the fearsome Battle of Bosworth Field. If popular legend is to be believed, in a fight to the death with Henry Tudor of the House of Lancaster, the crown, which Richard had worn into battle, fell from his head just before he was killed. Symbolically the crown was retrieved from a bush and placed upon his victorious opponent's head, ending the War of the Roses, fought between the Yorkists and the Lancastrians for thirty years.

To unite the two Houses the newly crowned King Henry the seventh went on to marry Elizabeth of York, and as the first Tudor King, chose a rose emblem that combined the red rose of Lancaster with the white rose of York.

As a new Royal Dynasty, the line of succession was extremely important, but it proved advantageous that Henry the 7th had produced an heir and a spare, because his eldest son, Arthur, died, and the title of Prince of Wales passed to his second son, Henry, along with Arthur's widow, Catherine of Aragon.

It was the Old King's dying wish that Henry the 8th should marry the Spanish born Catherine of Aragon, and the wedding took place just a fortnight before his coronation at Westminster Abbey in 1509. Catherine was older than her bridegroom, and a special dispensation had to be given by the Pope in Rome for the marriage to take place, even though Catherine declared that due to their youth, the union with Arthur had never been consummated.

At that time, Henry was nothing like the usual images we have of him in older age, being just eighteen, handsome, cultured and athletic. Queen Catherine without doubt adored him, and although aware that the King was often unfaithful to her, she remained constant to her husband her whole life long. It was an arrangement that would probably have suited both parties very well, had it not been for the fact that of the six children born to them, only one survived, with the added misfortune of being a girl. The Tudor Dynasty required certainty and the last time the crown had been destined for a female heir, Matilda, the result had been Civil War when her cousin Stephen usurped her.

As Catherine went beyond childbearing age, Henry turned to the Pope for an annulment believing that the marriage was cursed because his Queen had been his brother's widow. However, as the Vatican had allowed the union by virtue of a special dispensation to get around this in the first place, they were hardly going to agree with Henry, which would mean admitting they'd got it wrong. Never a man to accept "no" for an answer, Henry broke away from Rome, made himself head of a new protestant Church of England and granted himself a divorce so that he could marry Anne Boleyn, who was already expecting his child.

Although Catherine always refused to accept the divorce, despite being separated from her daughter and forced to live without the comforts she was used to, in her heart she believed Henry would return to her. When Anne's child proved to be another girl and efforts to produce a son were fruitless, the methods the desperate Queen is alleged to have employed to achieve this, resulted in her being sent to the Tower of London and executed for high treason in 1536, the year that the spurned Queen Catherine died.

As we all know Henry went on to marry again, and with his

next wife, Jane Seymour produced the son and heir the Tudor King had so longed for. Its possible love would have blossomed between them had she not died as a result of the birth, and the wives that followed failed to capture the ageing Henry's heart.

When Henry the 8th died his only son succeeded him; however, the Tudor line was anything but secure. The scramble for power was far from dignified and it was only when the crown finally reached Henry's daughter Elizabeth, the child of Anne Boleyn, that the stability of the Tudor Dynasty was assured.

Elizabeth 1st ruled for an incredible 45 years, and is a source of great fascination, not least because she chose never to marry. She was surrounded by suitors, yet steadfastly refused to make the ultimate commitment to any of them. At that time if she'd married, all her wealth, power and position would have passed to her husband, and she learnt while she was still very young that she was being targeted by men who coveted her power.

After Henry died the then Princess Elizabeth became the ward of her father's surviving wife, Catherine Parr. Interestingly when Henry had noticed Catherine, more for her compassion to care for him as his health deteriorated than for her sexual prowess, she had been in love with Thomas Seymour, the brother of Henry's third wife, Jane, but it would not have been wise for her to say no to the King!

So, not surprisingly within months of Henry's death, Catherine and Thomas married, giving Seymour intimate access to Elizabeth, and there is speculation that his attentions towards the young, impressionable girl were not altogether appropriate. When Catherine died in childbirth a year later, without doubt Thomas Seymour planned to marry the future Queen Elizabeth, but when this didn't work out, he changed tack and tried to kidnap Elizabeth's half-brother, the boy King Edward the 6th.

Consequently, Seymour was caught and sent to the Tower of

London on charges of high treason, where he was eventually executed, and Elizabeth was heard to comment, "Today died a man with much wit and not much judgement".

Elizabeth had perhaps had a lucky escape and was evidently very cautious when she came to the throne. Some have suggested that as the love of her life, Robert Dudley, Earl of Leicester, was already married, the new Queen vowed she would have no other husband. Also, her cousin Mary Queen of Scots had been turned into nothing more than a pawn in an elaborate and deadly political game as a result of an unwise marriage to Lord Darnley, and when he was eventually murdered, rather than learning from her mistakes, she made another equally disastrous marriage.

The consequence of this action was the imprisonment of the Scottish Queen by Elizabeth for almost 20 years, when she finally signed Mary's death warrant as her Catholic cousin had become too much of a threat and was alleged to be at the heart of conspiracy after conspiracy.

Whether Elizabeth was a virgin in the true sense of the word is impossible to say, even so, that she loved passionately is beyond question. But like the Elizabeth that would follow her, centuries later, this Tudor Queen put service to her people and her country first, and England prospered. What happened after her passing, even she could not control, although ironically Elizabeth named her cousin Mary Queen of Scot's only son, heir to her throne.

As any good history book will tell you, the Tudors were followed by the Stuarts, and although James 1st, son of Mary Queen of Scots united England and Scotland, both he and Charles 1st, the son who followed him, were clever men who proved to be disastrous Kings.

Charles 1st was a great believer in the divine right of Kings and refused to listen to Parliament, until of course it was too late. Led by Oliver Cromwell, the Parliamentarians launched a Civil War against the King and his Royalist supporters, which resulted in the execution of Charles 1st, leaving the nation subject to the puritanical protection of Oliver Cromwell, who even outlawed Christmas!

When the Commonwealth under Cromwell's control came to an end in 1660, the people of Britain were ready for some decadence and fun. When Charles 2nd returned from exile in France to be restored to the throne, the Merry Monarch, as the handsome Charles was known, led by example. He is most famous for having a succession of high-profile mistresses, but his favorite was without doubt the actress, Nell Gwynne. Instead of turning the people of Britain against him, Charles's popularity rose to new heights, for loving a commoner. It's alleged that on his deathbed the King's last words were "Let not poor Nellie starve", and Charles's successor, his brother James 2nd paid off Nell's mortgage, all her debts and granted her a substantial pension, which does add credence to the tale.

Despite Charles 2nd producing a plethora of illegitimate offspring, he lacked an heir apparent, which is why his brother succeeded him. However, this did weaken the House of Stuart considerably and after the demise of Charles 2nd's nieces, the people of Britain were told "Queen Anne's dead" and with her so was the Stuart hold on the throne.

And at last, we come to a genuine Royal love story, between a King and a Queen who met each other for the first time at St James's Palace, six hours before they were married in 1761. The bridegroom was King George 3rd of the Royal House of Hanover, and his bride was Princess Charlotte of Mecklenburg-Streliz. It seems the couple had similar tastes, sharing a love of the countryside, and the King, often known as "Farmer George", was fascinated by anything to do with agriculture.

The happy pair produced a huge family, consisting of fifteen children, and despite almost every King to have gone before him keeping a fine collection of mistresses, this deeply religious George remained faithful to Queen Charlotte throughout their marriage.

But if you're expecting a happy ending, you're going to be disappointed. In 1788 the King's behavior became very strange and many believed him to be mad. A later episode found him addressing a mighty oak tree as the King of Prussia, and eventually his eldest son, the future George 4th took over as Prince Regent in 1811. What it now appears he was suffering from was the physical illness, Porphyria, which manifested itself as madness, and as her husband faded before her eyes, the once gracious Queen Charlotte became increasingly depressed and died two years before George 3rd.

Now, although when it came to womanizing, as Prince Regent and then King, George 4th was notorious, and whether he ever actually found love is difficult to say. Ironically, his younger brother William, who succeeded him because George 4th had produced no legitimate heir, fared rather better in love, all be it, his liaisons were equally as scandalous.

William 4th was King for just six days short of seven years, and already 61 when he came to the throne. A Naval man known for his colorful language and a forthright lack of tact, despite the nickname "Silly Billy", endeared himself to the Great British people, being far more down to earth than his older brother.

And when it came to the ladies, like Charles 2nd, William had a very public affair with an actress, which lasted for twenty-two years and as depicted in a cartoon by the political satirist of the day, James Gilray, resulted in ten illegitimate children.

But there is another love story, which involves William, while still Duke of Clarence that is far less well known and our journal takes us to the beautiful county of Gloucestershire once again, to visit the magnificent Berkeley Castle. No stranger to Royal scandal this is where the unfortunate King Edward 2nd was murdered way back in the 14th Century, and throughout history this has been one ancestral seat with more than its fair share of colorful characters. And it was a very interesting Countess of Berkeley who is thought to have attracted the Duke of Clarence's attention back in the early 1800's.

Mary Cole was a butcher's daughter from Gloucester, who rose considerably above her station in life to marry Frederick Augustus, the 5th Earl of Berkely in 1796. However, several of their children were born well before this date, but it was claimed that an earlier wedding had taken place, generating considerable legal wrangling over the validity, and there were even suggestions that the Parish records in Berkeley's Church of St Mary were tampered with.

When the Earl died in 1810, while questions over which children were legitimate were being asked, Mary was evidently a very attractive widow.

This was at the time when the Prince of Wales became Prince Regent and a few years later, the future George 4th's only legitimate heir, Princess Charlotte, died in childbirth. It also coincided with a period of financial trouble for William, and with no heir apparent, the race was on amongst all the sons of George 3rd to come up with a healthy, legitimate offspring to carry on the line of succession.

William left the actress Dorothea Jordan, with whom he had ten children and started the search for a wealthy, suitable wife. The Countess of Berkeley had produced twelve children, so was obviously fertile, and it's highly likely that the lovely Mary was as down to earth as the Duke of Clarence was, and it's probable they would have done very well together.

But here's the irony! Although William had enjoyed a blissful existence with his actress mistress, not to mention the bedroom antics of his brother, the Prince Regent, it was felt the Countess of Berkeley would bring the monarchy into disrepute, because of the legitimacy issues connected with her children.

So, the future King William 4th married a suitable Princess, Adelaide of Saxe-Meiningen, but the two daughters the union produced, died in infancy, and the throne passed to William's 18-year-old niece, Victoria, daughter of his younger brother, the Duke of Kent, when he died in 1837.

Although the most perceived image we have of Queen Victoria is that of a stern, elderly lady dressed from head to toe in black, when she came to the throne, she was a lovely young girl, and immediately thoughts turned to finding a suitable bridegroom.

The preference for Victoria's first cousin, Prince Albert of Saxe-Coburg-Gotha was confirmed when the couple met for a second time in 1839, having first encountered each other three years earlier. Evidently the new Queen approved of Albert, describing him as "so sensible, so kind, so good and so amiable" with the added bonus of *"the most pleasing and delightful exterior and appearance you could possibly see."*

In fact the couple were married at St James's Palace on the 10th of February 1840, after Victoria had proposed to Albert, as protocol demanded on a reigning monarch.

Despite its undoubted convenience, this was a Royal marriage based on love, making it, as this journal has demonstrated, something of a rarity. Nine children were born to the happy couple between 1840 and 1857, as family values were restored to the nation after the long run of wild living Princes and Kings.

Today many of us associate this period of history with Christmas and we owe some of our best-loved seasonal traditions to the gifts bestowed by the German born Prince Albert upon his wife and family.

The most famous of these must be the Christmas tree, which Albert arranged as a special surprise. For centuries the Germans had decorated trees in a mid-winter festival, covering the bare branches of mighty oaks with brightly colored rags to encourage the tree spirits to return and make the leaves grow again.

Eventually with the arrival of Christianity, this practice was moved to Christmas, with a fir tree substituted for the oak thanks to its triangular shape, representing the father, son and Holy Ghost. Further adornments were added when the priest Martin Luther used candles on a fir tree for a special Christmas Eve service, and when Prince Albert presented his family with a beautifully decorated tree, it was an act of love and very romantic indeed.

When news of the Royal Christmas tree reached the people of Britain, the next year everybody wanted one, and since Victoria's reign, no traditional Christmas would be considered complete without a festively, decorated tree.

Where the Royal family led, the rest of the nation was bound to follow, and another of Prince Albert's loving gifts to Queen Victoria further encouraged a Great British summer tradition.

The concept of a seaside holiday had been popular since Georgian times, and Prince Albert was instrumental in creating the magnificent Osborne House on the Isle of Wight as a Royal seaside retreat for his hardworking wife.

The Isle of Wight became a popular destination for holidaymakers, but the Royal retreat remained extremely private, and even today you can still find evidence of how Victoria and Albert, accompanied by their children, enjoyed the pleasures of the Isle of Wight.

The nearest village to Osborne is Whippingham, and the magnificent church of St Mildred was where the Royal family worshiped when they were in residence. Also, the row of almshouses opposite the church were built on Queen Victoria's instructions for the retired Royal servants from the Osborne estate, making this a surprising find along an incredibly quiet, single track, country lane.

For Victorian visitors to the Isle of Wight the advent of steam and the creation of the railway provided a most popular means of transport, and Queen Victoria herself travelled by train around the Island. Part of the railway system has been preserved by the Isle of Wight Steam Railway Society, and with their prized collection of Victorian railway carriages, their headquarters at Haven Street is a delightful destination. However, you won't find any steam engines stopping at Whippingham, even though the station building still stands.

This was Queen Victoria and the Royal family's own private station in the 19th Century, and a short walk along the peace footpath will uncover traces of the old platform where once upon a time, not all that long ago, a happily married Royal couple alighted from a stylish carriage to hide from the world and enjoy a seaside holiday with their children.

With the strict demands of protocol, it must have been a strain at times for Prince Albert to be head of the household when his wife was the Queen, yet there are plenty of memorials to Prince Albert in his own right, with the grandest built upon the orders of Victoria.

If proof were needed that the Queen adored her husband, when this promising Royal love story came to a tragically abrupt end with Albert's death in 1861 at the age of 42, Victoria wore funeral black for the rest of her life.

For 13 years, Victoria went into deep mourning and refused to appear in public, retreating to Osborne and the other home

Prince Albert had rebuilt for her at Balmoral in Scotland, whenever she could. In fact, so complete was Victoria's withdrawal from her people, that there was even talk of the abolition of the monarchy.

But there was one man who is thought to have been instrumental in restoring Queen Victoria to her waiting public, a Scottish servant by the name of John Brown. Much has been written on the subject and it's alleged that there was even a secret marriage between this miss-matched couple, with satirists of the day referring to the Queen as "Mrs. Brown".

Whatever the true facts, Queen Victoria had a passionate love affair with Scotland, and even the Prime Ministers that served her were forced to travel north of the border on occasion to seek an audience with her majesty. Without doubt her favorite was Benjamin Disraeli, who she much preferred to his main rival William Gladstone, who she loathed. Although there is no suggestion of impropriety here, it does go to illustrate how Queen Victoria developed strong attachments to certain people, relying on them both personally and professionally.

Nevertheless, it was a lock of John Brown's hair that she allegedly requested her doctor place in her coffin, and when she died in 1901, the secret of whatever happened between the Queen and John Brown was buried with her.

Queen Victoria's fondness for her favorites and lack of amusement with those who displeased her is legendary, and even her own children were not exempt from her wrath. The Prince of Wales, her eldest son Bertie, was constantly out of favor with his mother, in part because she blamed him for the early death of his father, her beloved Prince Albert.

And when it came to the Prince of Wales's feelings for his mother, a lifetime facing her disapproval perhaps fueled his wild behavior rather than curbed it. In fact, when she died, one of the first things the 59-year-old did was give Osborne House to the nation, supposedly as a memorial to his mother. However, it's been suggested that the new King Edward 7th was thrilled to get rid of the house where he had been so dominated.

King Edward is perhaps best known for keeping a succession of glamorous mistresses, and whether he was truly in love with any woman is very hard to judge. No doubt the most eminent psychiatrist of the day, Sigmund Freud would have had much to say on the subject, but although the King may have struggled with love, he certainly inspired it in others, namely his people, his mistresses and most of all his wife, Queen Alexandra.

Whatever her husband's well-publicized misdemeanors, the elegant and dignified Danish Princess he had had the good sense to marry, stood resolutely at his side, taking consolation in the fact that she believed the King always loved her best.

Moving into the early 20th Century, one of the most famous Royal romances of all time resulted in a marriage, but also threatened the monarchy and brought about the abdication of King Edward 8th in 1936.

The object of Edward's affections was an American divorcee, Wallis Simpson, who he was determined to marry as soon as she was free. Britain as a nation was shocked and felt that the American socialite had stolen their King. Some suggest that Edward had found a convenient way of shirking his Royal duties, while others are of the opinion that this was indeed true love, and the King had been braver than those of his predecessors who had settled for a marriage of convenience and a string of mistresses. As Duke and Duchess of Windsor, Edward and Wallis lived in exile in Paris and were only parted when the duke died from throat cancer in 1972.

As our time looking at Royal Romances draws to a close, we couldn't possibly conclude without considering the most widely publicized Royal Romance of all time, between Charles, His Royal Highness, the Prince of Wales and Lady Diana Spencer.

Ironically, had Edward the eighth ruled as King, married a suitable lady and produced an heir, Prince Charles may never have found himself first in line to the British throne.

When he was just three years old, his mother became Queen Elizabeth 2nd, and by the time the prince had come of age, every press agency in the world was speculating about who the eligible young Royal would marry.

Prince Charles certainly seemed to be in no hurry to find a bride, but shortly after his 30th birthday, he met the shy, youngest daughter of Earl Spencer of Althorp, Lady Diana.

With an impeccable ancestry, Diana had been born on the Royal Estate at Sandringham, before moving to Althorp in Northamptonshire, when her father inherited the title, Earl Spencer. After a brief spell at finishing school, Diana bought herself a flat in fashionable Fulham and flourished as a children's nanny, a job that she loved.

Before long it wasn't only Prince Charles who had been captivated by Diana; the British public started a love affair with the future Princess of Wales that would last for all time.

It was a 20th Century fairy story come true, and when Diana left Buckingham Palace, a lady, to marry her Prince Charming under the huge dome of St Paul's Cathedral on the 29th of July 1981, she returned a Princess, to the delight of the cheering crowds. London was in party mood to celebrate the Royal wedding that heralded a new age in the history of the British monarchy.

In a few short years, the new Princess of Wales blossomed into a delightful young woman, with a unique style of her own, and after the birth of two sons, Princes William and Harry, had secured the succession, Diana had fulfilled one of her most important Royal duties as a future Queen.

But things were not all that they might have seemed, and eventually both Buckingham Palace and the British government had to admit that the romance was over, and the Prince and Princess of Wales were divorced in 1996.

And as we all know, this was not the end of the story. Even stripped of her HRH status, Diana, Princess of Wales was still adored wherever she went, and for just the briefest of moments it appeared that she was succeeding in building a new life for herself.

Then tragedy struck on a Paris night in August 1997, when Diana was killed in a car crash, along with her companion Dodi Al Fahed and their driver. The outpouring of public grief and the dignified funeral of the young woman who had changed the face of British Royalty proved beyond question just how adored Diana had been, and when she was finally laid to rest on a peaceful island in the middle of the Oval Lake at Althorp, her ancestral home, the nation vowed never to forget Diana, Princess of Wales.

It is a promise that has been kept, and as the years go by, visitors to Althorp in Northamptonshire and the London residences that Diana called home, from the charming flat in Coleherne Court to the regal elegance of Kensington Palace, we are constantly reminded that Diana, the People's Princess once passed this way.

The fairy tale may not have ended as everyone, not least, Charles and Diana, had hoped, but this story none the less qualifies as a Royal Romance of its time.

Throughout history there have been many more Royal Romances than those featured in this journal, and in truth, so long as the monarchy survives, there will be many more to come. Ironically it isn't only the members of the Royal families of the past for whom true love ran smoothly who are most fondly remembered, because just as is the case in popular novels, when it comes to romance, whether Royal or otherwise, there's always room for secrets and intrigue, alongside the hearts and flowers.

❖ ❖ ❖

ROYAL SCANDALS & CONSPIRACIES

There are some who would argue that in the 21st Century a monarchy, of any description, is an outdated institution, but paradoxically, it only takes the merest hint of a Royal scandal or conspiracy for the world press to be in hot pursuit of the story. What's more, any newspaper or magazine fortunate enough to get a Royal exclusive, even in our modern age, is guaranteed to increase circulation dramatically, suggesting that there is as much interest in the monarchy as there has ever been.

So how did it all begin? Well, for the British, the answer to that question is quite simply when the first Kings and Queens emerged from the warring tribes of ancient times to wear a crown and sit upon a throne. However, they had to do a great deal more than that!

Kings, or Queens for that matter, had to be fierce warriors, not only to seize power, but also to withstand challenges from their fellow countrymen and foreign invaders, and the term "Hostile Takeover", back then, precisely meant that.

In today's multi-cultural society, we can all claim very different ancestries, and whether black haired, dark-eyed Celts, blonde haired, blue-eyed Anglo-Saxons, or in more recent times of Asian and African extraction, the melting pot of diverse peoples that make up the British Isles, creates an ever-changing anthropological landscape.

The first invaders to really make an impact were the Romans who arrived in force in 43 AD.

The Ancient Britons fought hard to resist, the most remembered being the mighty warrior Queen Boudicca, who certainly gave the Romans a very tough time, even though it was to no avail. But there was little conspiracy or scandal at play; these were brutal times, where rising to power was a dangerous business and if someone was plotting against you, little was done to hide it.

Nevertheless, the Romans were an altogether more sophisticated bunch than the Ancient Britons, and you only have to look at their legacy of long straight roads, fine architecture and beautiful baths to appreciate this, and when it came to conspiracies, they were centuries ahead of their time. As we all know, Julius Caesar, who first set foot in Britain before the main Roman invasion crying, *"I came, I saw, I conquered"*, in fact he came to nothing more than a very sorry end, stabbed to death on the steps of the forum in Rome, by those he had thought were his closest friends.

Eventually, the scandals and conspiracies in the Roman Empire, which were as lethal as they were legendary, proved to be a major factor in Rome's downfall, and as they departer Britain's shores in the 5th Century AD, there were other invaders ready to take their place.

The first of these were the Saxons, and it took them just over two centuries to force the native Celts out of England, into Scotland and Wales, before splitting the nation further, into Seven Kingdoms. This was still a bloodthirsty age and each successive King fought for dominance over his neighbors, until finally Egbert of Wessex became the first acknowledged King of all England in

829.

When Egbert died, he was succeeded by his sons and grandsons; rather than the Seven Kingdoms once again going into battle for supremacy, and the concept of a line of succession has been an integral part of the monarchy ever since. But naturally because there were plenty of would-be Kings who were not the Heir Apparent, or even the Heir Presumptive, the motivation for some of the greatest scandals and conspiracies in the history books took shape alongside the notion of a hereditary monarchy.

As the centuries past, and the Anglo-Saxon Kings were toppled by marauding Vikings, only to be restored to the throne again, some monarchs proved excellent, while others were worse than useless. However, the next big change came when King Edward, the Confessor, died in 1066.

Although you might not know much about this King, the date will be very familiar as the year of The Battle of Hastings, which came about because, Edward, who died childless, allegedly promised the English throne to two different people, his brother-in-law Harold, (who the conspiracy theorists believe the Old King disliked intensely) and his distant cousin, William, Duke of Normandy.

Quickly Harold stormed to power, but when William brought an invasion force from France, to dispute the succession, he defeated Harold at the Battle of Hastings, and the Norman Conquests changed the face of Britain and the aristocracy beyond recognition. William I, or the Conqueror, as he's better known, surrounded himself with Norman Nobles, but subduing the English was no easy task, and he still had his lands in Normandy to oversee. In fact, he died in France, while attacking the city of Nantes.

Now, as you might guess, tact and diplomacy did not play a huge part in the Norman Conquests, but William 1st, like all his predecessors had a big problem. He couldn't live forever. Unlike Edward the Confessor though, he had an heir, and several other sons, but he thought the eldest wasn't tough enough to rule England, so he chose William, his third son to succeed him.

A recipe for conspiracy if ever there was one, William the 2nd died under very suspicious circumstances, and was succeeded very speedily by his brother, Henry 1st, whose reign ended when *he* died of food poisoning. It is believed Henry may have been involved in William's death, but this early history proves beyond doubt than when the succession isn't clearly defined, there's always going to be trouble.

For most people, the best-known example of Royal brothers conspiring and fighting amongst themselves to decide who should become King is that of Richard the Lionheart and his brother John, not least because of their appearance in the legend of Robin Hood.

Part of the problem in this instance was the refusal of their father, King Henry 2nd, to name his heir, setting son against son, as conspiracy became as important a part of the line of succession as birthright. Matters were further aggravated because the mother of both Richard and John, Eleanor of Aquitaine, wasn't averse to taking sides, and as her marriage to their father had deteriorated into a veritable warzone, she actively encouraged Richard, her favourite, to take up arms against his father.

When Henry 2nd died at the French Castle of Chinon in 1189, he'd finally named Richard, his third son, as his heir, and so began a period of history dominated by Crusader Knights, Holy Quests and ubiquitous Damsels in Distress.

The legend of Robin Hood tells the story of the noble Robin of Loxley, a supporter of King Richard the Lionheart and his Crusades to the Holy Land. When Robin returned from the Crusades, he found that King Richard's brother, John, had taken charge of the country, raising taxes to fill his own pockets, leaving the English people facing extreme poverty and starvation. And to make matters worse, Prince John and his greedy nobles had confiscated the lands of those away fighting the Crusades with King Richard, including of course, the property of Robin of Loxley.

Robin turned outlaw to wreak revenge on John, and joined together with other likeminded outlaws in Sherwood Forest, plotting to remove the usurping Prince from power and restore King Richard's throne. Robin, his band of Merry Men, and the fair Maid Marian, stole from the rich; namely Prince John and his cronies, to give to the poor; the wronged citizens of the nation.

Eventually, just in the nick of time, King Richard returned to send his wicked brother packing, and Richard's grateful subjects rejoiced at their liberation from Prince John's tyranny.

It's a wonderful story and has become so much a part of popular culture that Richard the Lionheart has gone down in history as one of the greatest Kings of all time, while his brother John, who did succeed Richard after his death in 1199, is often referred to as Bad King John. However, delve a little deeper and you will find a very different version of events.

Richard the Lionheart ruled England for ten years but was only ever actually in the country for a total of seven months. It was Richard and not John who raised most of the taxes, to fund the crusades and pay for his ransom when he managed to get himself captured by the Emperor of Germany. Whether Prince John, as he then was, played any part in the abduction of his brother is frequently speculated about, but has never been proved, and as Richard failed to produce an heir, (no doubt as a direct result of always being away fighting or in prison) the crown eventually passed to John anyway.

If John did conspire against his brother Richard, when he came to the throne, he certainly got a taste of his own medicine, when the nobility rebelled against him, forcing the signing of the Magna Carta, which prohibited any abuse of Royal power by King John, or future monarchs, and this, in real history books rather than the Tales of Robin Hood, is what he is most remembered for.

To say that Richard the Lionheart wasn't all good and King John, wasn't all bad, is probably the fairest assessment of these two kings.

However, as we all love a courageous, handsome hero and a deliciously, evil villain, chances are that the legend, as told in Robin Hood, will live on, because inevitably the truth will never be allowed to get in the way of this particularly good story.

Having explored the scandal and conspiracy of sibling rivalry, we move on in time to the grandson of King John, and a family history with far too many skeletons in the cupboard. Our story begins with the father of this unhappy dynasty, Edward 1st, who became King in 1272. At two meters tall, he was nicknamed "Longshanks", as he stood head and shoulders above most of his countrymen and was without doubt a warrior King. Near neighbors Scotland and Wales certainly discovered this to their cost, and Edward's deviousness and brutality have become legendary, in part due to the success of the blockbuster movie, "Braveheart", which tells the story of William Wallace and his valiant attempt to liberate Scotland from English rule.

But again, when we come to the question of the succession, the son, who Longshanks created Prince of Wales in 1301, had always been something of a disappointment to his confrontational father. Edward the 2nd could not have been more different from Edward 1st, and with the benefit of hindsight, his homosexuality was a major factor in the troubles that beset him. Warring with Scotland was of little interest to him, and after his father's death, when the Scots took on the English at the Battle of

Bannockburn, Edward's army was beaten, and the independence of Scotland assured.

And so, we come to Berkeley Castle in Gloucestershire, where Edward 2nd was brutally murdered in the most horrific circumstances. Expected to do his duty, Edward married Isabella of France, and despite his obvious preference for male company, the union produced four children. However, Isabella has gone down in history as a woman scorned, and when she took her revenge on Edward 2nd, the fury of hell would have been mild by comparison.

When Isabella fell in love with Roger Mortimer, a sworn enemy of the King, the trouble really started. The pair deposed Edward, had him imprisoned in a cell at Berkeley Castle, and seized power in the name of the heir apparent, who would later become Edward 3rd.

The King's closest male friends were murdered, and when Edward 2nd failed to die quietly as a result of the noxious fumes from the rubbish pit below his prison cell, he was "traditionally disemboweled" on the orders of his wife, this conventional and gruesome death preserved for homosexuals back in the 14th Century.

Ironically when Edward the third was old enough to seize power back from his mother, he went on to become a very good King, but when it comes to scandal and conspiracy, it is another Edward, this time the 5th, who is at the heart of a mystery, still unsolved to this day.

A visit to the Tower of London will reveal the sad tale of the Two Princes, one of whom was destined to be Edward the 5th, who with his younger brother was in the care of their Uncle Richard, the Duke of Gloucester. On his deathbed, King Edward 4th appointed Richard England's Protector, and the evidence suggests this would, to use a biblical analogy, have been like entrusting the care of the newborn baby Jesus to King Herod.

The two princes were last seen in September 1483, at the Tower, and the finger of suspicion pointed accusingly at their uncle, the Duke of Gloucester, who in the absence of the princes, became King Richard 3rd.

Some argue that history has unfairly maligned Richard 3rd, and William Shakespeare's play on the subject did little for the King's PR. But for those who believe in divine justice, his reign lasted just two years, before he was killed at the Battle of Bosworth Field in 1485.

The man responsible for the demise of Richard took the empty throne of England and began a new Royal House, as Henry 7th, the first of the Tudor Kings. However, although more than capable of scheming and conniving in his own right, it was his second son, Henry who turned Royal scandal and conspiracy into an art-form.

Although looking at the history books, it appears that Henry 8th was obsessed with women, it was in fact the old problem of the succession and producing a healthy male heir that pre-occupied him most. When Henry became King, he inherited the widow of his older brother Arthur, Catherine of Aragon, and a special dispensation from the Pope in Rome allowed them to marry.

Sadly, for Henry, Catherine failed to produce a son, and despite numerous pregnancies her only child to survive was a girl, Mary.

By this time Henry realized that Catherine's childbearing days were over and turned his attention to the young and bewitching Anne Boleyn. Henry now wanted the Pope to overturn his agreement to the marriage with Catherine, so there could be an annulment and the King would be able to marry Anne.

The Pope however refused, so Henry decided to break from

Rome, become head of a new protestant Church of England, and grant himself a divorce, after which he married Anne, who was already pregnant. But after all that effort, Anne's child was a girl, Elizabeth, and despite Henry hoping future pregnancies would result in a son, nature did not oblige, and Anne was swiftly despatched, accused of adultery and beheaded.

Henry's next choice of wife *did* produce a son, but as she died as a result of the achievement, Henry continued to marry and divorce or behead at will, having an incredible six wives in all, before his own death in 1547.

With a new church and boy King, Henry's hopes of a secure succession were left unrealized when Edward 6th died in 1553 at the age of 15, and the Catholics, who had constantly plotted to restore England to Rome were ready to support Henry's eldest daughter Mary, a devout Catholic in a bid for the throne.

The Protestants however fought back, manipulating the 16-year-old Lady Jane Grey onto the throne of England, but the unfortunate girl, merely a pawn in an elaborate conspiracy, was deposed by Mary after just nine days, and sent to the Tower of London as a traitor, where she was later executed.

For the Protestants "Bloody" Mary, as the new Queen became known, lived up to her name, executing as heretics those who refused to convert back to Rome. Plots and conspiracies sprang up everywhere, and as Mary's marriage to Philip of Spain failed to produce any issue, the Catholics feared that their power would die with Mary.

While Mary was still alive, the Catholics had urged the Queen to execute her half-sister, Elizabeth, the Protestant daughter of Anne Boleyn, and the younger girl had shown courage beyond her years when she was imprisoned in the Tower of London. Nevertheless, Mary died before any death warrant could be signed, and Queen Elizabeth I began her reign in 1558, declaring religious tolerance. But as the Catholic conspiracies grew ever bolder, fear for her throne made Elizabeth outlaw Catholicism, and just as in Mary's reign, many lost their lives for their beliefs.

Even so, Catholic priests still travelled in secret around the country, and many of the large houses, where families stayed true to Rome, constructed priest holes, where a man could be concealed, if they were raided when mass was being said. A fine example is Harvington Hall where there are priest holes in almost every room, and many priests were hidden here during this period of Catholic persecution.

Elizabeth's greatest fear was that the Catholic Queen of Scots, her cousin Mary, who had been crowned while still a babe in arms, would make an attempt for the English throne, as another pawn in the hands of powerful conspirators. It did not help that when she grew up Mary was prone to making disastrous marriages, something that Elizabeth avoided altogether.

Sadly, when Mary threw herself on Elizabeth's mercy, the Catholic conspirators were still waiting in the wings, and after years spent moving the Scottish Queen from Castle to Castle, Elizabeth ordered Mary's execution, convinced she was guilty of treason.

Elizabeth, as the Virgin Queen, ruled England for an incredible 45 years, but the downside of self-inflicted spinsterhood was the distinct lack of an heir. Ironically, the son of Mary Queen of Scots became James 1st, uniting England and Scotland, as the first Stuart King in 1603.

And still the conspiracies over religion continued, as in 1605 the Catholic Guy Fawkes, attempted to blow up the Houses of Parliament with the King inside. However, as we all celebrate burning "Guy Fawkes" on bonfire night every November 5th, the gunpowder plot clearly failed.

As the century progressed and James 1st was succeeded by his son Charles 1st, England was plunged into Civil War, when Oliver Cromwell and his Parliamentarians challenged the divine Right of Kings. The upshot was that Charles was beheaded, and Cromwell made himself Lord Protector, until Charles 2nd was restored to the throne, returning in 1660 from exile in France.

During Cromwell's Puritan years there was little opportunity for scandalous behaviour; he even cancelled Christmas, but Charles 2nd certainly put the "merry" back into "monarch", as this is how he became known. There were scandals a plenty, which were at times controversial, but his love for his favorite mistress, the actress Nell Gwynne, only endeared him to his people. Charles' dying words were allegedly "Let not poor Nellie starve" and as he set a precedent for very public Royal affairs, the stage was set for a new era.

The Stuart line came to an end in 1714, by which time the Act of Settlement had been passed, ensuring the succession remained Protestant, and as the German House of Hanover provided the nearest relations to fit the bill, George 1st arrived from Germany to take the throne, unable to even speak English!

For many people in the newly United Kingdom, this was not a popular choice, and a Jacobite rising in Scotland, fueled by the Catholic members of the Stuart line, unhappy about their exclusion from the line of succession, served notice that more trouble was ahead. It was actually in George 2nd's reign that the Stuart, Bonnie Prince Charlie marched an army of fierce Scots south towards London, only to turn back on the advice of turncoat spies, to face defeat on the bloody battlefield of Culloden.

The next George, the third, was without doubt the best of the bunch, but sadly ill health has meant he has gone down in history as having been mad. However, in a journal about scandal and conspiracy, it is his eldest son George who proved to be something of an expert!

As a young man, the Prince of Wales was handsome and dashing, but his father despaired of his behavior. He ran up colossal debts, gambling and entertaining, and he regularly featured in the newspapers of the day because of his scandalous affairs with a succession of mistresses. In fact, in 1785, after failing to seduce a Catholic lady who had taken his fancy, he actually married her, quite illegally, in order to win her over. The lady in question, Maria Fitzherbert is perhaps the best known of George's mistresses, not least because of the property he bought in the seaside resort of Brighton to house his secret bride.

Just as the Georgians flocked to the Spas of Bath and Cheltenham to take the health-giving waters, they also believed sea bathing to be equally efficacious and seaside resorts were developing at a rapid pace. George 3rd had a fondness for Weymouth, but his son chose Brighton, as far away from his father as possible, whether at the seaside, or at court in London. However, when the Prince of Wales called on the services of architect John Nash, the man responsible for many of Bath's beautiful buildings, to renovate the secret hideaway, it became anything but inconspicuous.

The exotic Palace, complete with onion domes and spires took thirty-five years to create, and today visitors to Brighton Pavilion can still marvel at the opulence and extravagance of this spectacularly spendthrift Prince of Wales.

Interestingly, architect John Nash also transformed Buckingham Palace, when the prince became King George 4th in 1820. George 3rd had bought Buckingham House with a view to creating an alternative Royal residence to St James's Palace, which he described as a "dust trap", but became ill before he could begin renovations.

John Nash took almost twenty years to complete the project and the amount of time he was kept busy at both Brighton Pavilion and Buckingham Palace fuelled considerable gossip, as it has been suggested that George 4th had a great fondness for the gentleman's wife!

The only reason that George, while still Prince of Wales was prevailed upon to marry a "suitable" bride was the fact that Parliament agreed to pay off his enormous debts if he did so. His marriage to Mrs. Fitzherbert ten years earlier, as we know, was illegal, so nothing stood in the way. But when he met his new bride to be, Caroline of Brunswick, he evidently wished that someone would come up with just cause why they should not be lawfully joined together at the wedding ceremony. The couple hated each other on sight, and although the marriage was consummated, producing a daughter, they were unable to live together, and over the years the infidelities of both parties were sensationally reported in the press.

We know that public opinion turned against the future George 4th because of his treatment of his wife, and when Caroline wrote to the newspapers to give her version of events, the novelist Jane Austen commented upon the situation in one of her letters saying:

> "I suppose all the world is sitting in judgement on the Princess of Wales's letter, poor woman, I shall support her as long as I can, because she is a woman, and because I hate her husband."

Stern words indeed, and as George 4th turned from a handsome youth into a grossly overweight, dissolute man because of overindulgence, his health deteriorated, and as his only legitimate daughter, Princess Charlotte, pre-deceased him, when he died, the throne passed to his younger, (but not by much) brother.

When it came to scandal, William 4th had led equally as colorful a life as George 4th. As Duke of Clarence, William had lived with the actress Dorothea Jordan for 22 years and they had ten children, all of whom were of course illegitimate. Like his older brother, his financial troubles let him to marry a "suitable" bride and as Princess Charlotte, George 4th's heir, had died in childbirth , the race was on between the lesser royals to come up with a legitimate offspring. But well into his fifties, despite his younger bride, there was no surviving issue.

When William became King in 1830, he was 64, and with the nickname "Silly Billy", you can immediately work out how his public perceived him, and when he died in 1837, the British people must have wondered what manner of monarch the House of Hanover would produce next. From the madness of the much-loved George 3rd and the much-hated reprobate George 4th, right through to "Silly Billy" William 4th, the prospect was far from promising. However, waiting in the wings was a young girl, just eighteen years of age, about to turn around the reputation of this Royal house.

We are of course talking about Queen Victoria, possibly the most respectable of all British monarchs.

With the restoration of moral behavior, Victoria led by example, marrying her beloved Prince Albert in 1840, and producing a secure succession of nine children, including four sons.

Now, you may be wondering how Queen Victoria's exemplary good name could possibly be associated with either scandal or conspiracy but travel back in time to the autumn of 1888 and the London slums of Whitechapel, and you will uncover an intriguing Royal conspiracy that is still a source of frenzied speculation to this very day.

When a woman's body was discovered on the 7th of August 1888 in Gunthorpe Street, that back then was known as George Yard, nobody really paid much attention. The attack on Martha Tabram had been brutal, she'd been stabbed thirty-nine times in the throat, chest and abdomen, but this was one of the most deprived districts of the city; murder was commonplace, and an occupational hazard for prostitutes; Martha's unfortunate profession.

Then on August 31st, in Buck's Row, now Durward Street, another woman's body was discovered. Polly Nichols was also a prostitute, and although the cause of death was most likely strangulation, her throat had been slashed from ear to ear and her body horribly mutilated.

Only when Annie Chapman's body was discovered on September 8th in Hanbury Street did alarm bells start to ring. Annie too had been a prostitute, and with her throat cut and intestines ripped out, fears that a brutal serial killer was on the loose became widespread.

The police did what they could, but progress was slow and when a letter arrived on the 27th of September written in blood and claiming to be the culprit, signed Jack the Ripper, an evil killer became a press sensation and a household name.

Weeks passed and all went relatively quiet until on the night of 30th September, when two more prostitutes were found murdered, quite literally within hours of each other.

The first, known as Long Liz had had her throat cut, but the second, Catherine Eddowes, found in Mitre Square, was horribly mutilated with body parts, including a kidney, removed.

The murders were becoming more horrendous and when the body of Mary Kelly was discovered on the 9th of November, her mutilated body was unrecognisable. The scene of crime images are as truly appalling to look at today as they were back in 1888, and the police search for Jack the Ripper intensified.

Mary Kelly is officially the last of the Jack the Ripper murders and the identity of the killer has never been uncovered, although many theories have been put forward over the years.

And this, quite incredibly, is where Queen Victoria has become a part of the Ripper legend, to such a degree, that there have even been those who have suggested that Jack the Ripper was none other than the Queen herself.

In all the many thousands of books written about Jack the Ripper since that fateful autumn of 1888, little credence has been given to the theory that the Royal grandmother was stalking the streets of Whitechapel, killing and mutilating prostitutes.

However, the conspiracy theorists have a much more believable version of events that puts Queen Victoria and members of her household under the spotlight, most significantly the Royal Physician, Sir William Gull.

Queen Victoria's grandson, Prince Albert Victor was destined to become the heir apparent, as the eldest male child of her first-born son, the future Edward the 7th. Many in the family, including Queen Victoria and the boy's father seem to have thought him to be retarded, but that did not prevent him from being connected to several scandals, including fathering an illegitimate son, and involvement in the Cleveland Street Scandal, where police uncovered a male brothel.

However, the most publicized story about him came to prominence in the 1960s and 70s, which connected the Royal grandson to the Ripper murders. Prince Albert Victor, or so the story goes, was sent to the Whitechapel studios of artist Walter Sickert to learn how to paint. While there he fell in love with one of Sickert's models, a common shop girl, who he married in secret and had a child with.

The hypothesis was that one of the witnesses at the wedding was Mary Kelly, a friend of the bride, who upon recognizing the

Royal bridegroom attempted to blackmail the government. As a trusted Royal servant, Sir William Gull was dispatched to murder Kelly and all those she shared the information with, namely the other Ripper victims, and make it look like the work of a madman.

The explanation for the night of the double murder was mistaken identity, which is why Long Liz was not mutilated, but the whole Ripper and the Royals story is frequently put down to urban legend, and of course has provided the plot for any number of Jack the Ripper movies.

Prince Albert Victor died, quite unexpectedly, just four years after the Ripper murders at the age of twenty-eight, with the cause of death given as flu. But this is perhaps where the real Royal conspiracy lies.

There are three other alternatives given for what might have happened to the unfortunate Prince, the first being that he died of Syphilis as a result of his dissipated lifestyle.

The second option is rather more sinister, as rumours spread that he had been given an overdose of morphine, to avoid an unsuitable heir succeeding to the throne, and lastly, the most bizarre option suggesting that the "death" story was a cover up for the prince's madness, with the young man being dispatched to an asylum on the Isle of Wight, where he allegedly lived unseen, until his death in the 1920s.

Whatever the truth behind all these conspiracy theories, their association with Queen Victoria is fascinating, and even if nothing more than over imaginative flights of fancy, the stories show a very dark side of Victorian London, not so far removed from the magnificent façade of Buckingham Palace.

As we have now travelled at great speed through history, a pattern has emerged when a monarch is on the throne for a very long time, and a Prince of Wales is kept in waiting.

It was true in George 4th's case, and as Queen Victoria ruled Britannia for an incredible sixty-three years and seven months, her eldest son had to wait until he was 59 to take on the role, he had been preparing for all his life.

After the stern morality, on the surface at least of the Victorian age, the dawn of the Edwardian era, which began when the Queen died in 1901, couldn't have been more different. The new King, who greatly enjoyed his country estate at Sandringham, was nevertheless at the heart of every grand, glittering society occasion, and just as had been the case when he was Prince of Wales, wherever Edward 7th was to be found, scandal was never too far away.

In the early days, to try and curb the wild behaviour of the Prince of Wales, Queen Victoria decided he should be married as quickly as possible to a suitable Princess, and Alexandra of Denmark was selected. Fortunately for the Prince, Alexandra was beautiful and affectionate, but unable to control her young husband's wild ways, especially with the ladies, she tolerated his affairs. When asked in later years about this she always replied that he loved her best, and the truth is, he probably did.

Even so, throughout his entire married life Edward the 7th kept numerous mistresses. Actresses like Lillie Langtry and Sarah Bernhardt along with various socialites including the famous American beauty Jennie Jerome, later Lady Randolph Churchill and mother of Britain's World War II Prime Minister, Winston, were great favorites.

In fact, his last mistress, Alice Keppel was even admitted by Queen Alexandra to Buckingham Palace to be at the King's deathbed in 1910.

Now, as we already know, King Edward's eldest son, Prince

Albert Victor died at the age of twenty-eight, shortly after the Ripper murders, and the throne passed to Edward's second son who became King George 5th.

The people of Britain felt a great sense of loss at the old King's passing despite all the scandals, and as the new King enjoyed a contented married life with Queen Mary, the Princess who had been his older brother's fiancée at the time of his death, the years between 1910 and 1936 were characterized by dignified Royal stability.

But with World War II looming large when George 5th died, the Prince of Wales in waiting had an even greater bombshell to drop on the people of Britain. Like other monarchs before him George 5th was aware of his eldest son's shortcomings, and even warned Prime Minister Stanley Baldwin that after becoming King, "the boy" would ruin himself in twelve months. This was a prophecy that proved to be truer than he could possibly have known.

Edward 8th became King on 20th January 1936, and a scandal even bigger than the affairs of Edward 7th rocked the nation. The King announced his intention to marry his American mistress, the already twice married divorcee, Wallis Simpson, provoking a constitutional crisis that was only resolved by Edward's abdication on the 11th of December.

Just as his father had predicted, Edward 8th had lasted as King slightly less than the twelve months, but as his brother stepped forward to become King George 6th, at least the monarchy, although seriously shaken by the abdication, was able to survive.

Through the hard years of World War II, George 6th and his family stood shoulder to shoulder with their fellow Londoners, as Hitler's Luftwaffe blitzed the city with nightly bombing raids.

Then when the war was over the Royal family celebrated with

their people as a new age of hope dawned. George 6th and his wife, Queen Elizabeth had restored the nation's faith in the monarchy and when the King died as a result of ill health in 1952, his eldest daughter, as Elizabeth the 2nd, came to the throne equipped with a sense of duty and willingness to serve beyond her very real 25 years.

And so in the final years of the 20th Century, with millennium celebrations on the horizon, a Royal tragedy occurred that once again threw the monarchy into disarray, resulting in conspiracy theories threatening far reaching consequences for the constitutional monarchy.

When Queen Elizabeth attended the wedding of her eldest son Prince Charles to Lady Diana Spencer at St Paul's Cathedral in 1981, it must have been with a degree of relief that the succession was going to be safe. Like so many Princes of Wales to have gone before him, Charles had been involved with several young ladies, some of whom had been a great deal more suitable than others. At the age of 33 it seemed Charles had at last found his very own fairytale Princess to be a mother to his children and eventually become his Queen.

But sadly, this is one fairytale without a happy ending and by the 1990s the delightful family snapshots of the "Wales's" with their two sons, Princes William and Harry were nothing more than a façade.

The very public separation and then divorce of the Prince and Princess of Wales in 1996, meant that the couple's private affairs were splashed right across the media, and the people of Britain's adoration of Diana, Princess of Wales resulted in a significant downturn in the popularity of the "Royal Family Firm".

News that the Prince of Wales had conducted a long-term affair with Mrs. Camilla Parker-Bowles turned public opinion further against him, and Diana continued to be the most popular Royal, even though her HRH status had been taken from her.

Ironically, the situation was far more complex and there were faults on both sides, but for the die-hard conspiracists, the fact that Camilla also happens to be the great-granddaughter of Alice Keppel, the Royal mistress allowed to be at the deathbed of Edward 7th, history has indeed repeated itself.

Whatever the wrongs or rights of the much-publicized break up of Diana and Charles, when news came through that Diana had been killed as the result of a car crash in a Paris tunnel in the early hours of the 31st August 1997, the nation was first plunged into a state of shock and then into a state of grief and mourning.

Although the findings suggest this was a tragic accident, how or why the Princess came to be killed so unexpectedly has continued to be subject to both intense investigation and even greater speculation, with conspiracy theories around every corner you turn. But as Diana, Princess of Wales rests in peace on an island at Althorp, her ancestral home, who can say what the future will reveal about this ongoing Royal saga, and for that matter any of the other scandals and conspiracies featured in this history journal.

Like the memory of Diana, Princess of Wales, a good story never dies, and down through the ages, it only improves with keeping, and of course re-telling.

◆ ◆ ◆

Author's note 2022:
As a footnote to this journal, when I was flying over Althorp Park to get aerial footage for a Diana documentary, the local helicopter pilot informed me that Diana was NOT buried on the Althorp Island as publicly stated.

Rather, she had been "secretly interned" at the family crypt in the local church during the hours of darkness, confirmed by witnesses to the night-time disturbances. Followed up by a report of fresh, wet mortar on the tomb itself the following day.

The ploy of advising the public that her remains were ensconced on the island inside the estate; an attempt to reduce pressure on the church itself as a shrine for visiting loyalist and Diana followers.

Yet another conspiracy theory? Who knows, but I find helicopter pilots, intelligent and usually reliable sources of information. We "buzzed" Althorp for just a few minutes as the occupants tend to complain at aerial intrusion. As well as ground-based incursions. I will not be visiting with a spade.

16/2/22 - Footnote; As of this week, Prince Andrew has settled by undisclosed sum, a case brought in civil court against him for various actual crimes in American law. THUS avoiding a trial by jury days after he insisted on his right to have one.

Time will tell, if this was a prudent investment to try and close a chapter on this the LATEST Royal Scandal, OR in fact a payment in lieu of being found guilty of the offences claimed.

PRINCESS DIANA

1961-1997

In fairy tales dreams do come true; little girls can grow up to marry handsome Princes, and live happily ever after in beautiful palaces, where they have delightful children of their own, and in time become Queen, to rule with wisdom and grace. But in real life, even when it appears a fairy tale is being played out in the full glare of our modern media age, things never seem to go quite to plan.

There are few places in the world today where you still find Princes and Princesses, or for that matter Kings and Queens, but the thousands of visitors who travel to London each year come face to face with Royal Palaces and a history of succession that dates right back to the dark ages. However, in the late summer of 1997 people from all over the world gathered in London, in a state of utter shock and disbelief, as the most publicised fairy tale of the 20th Century came to an abrupt and tragic end.

In the early hours of Sunday the 31st of August, a shocking news story began to unfold, with the world's press agencies on red alert. Shortly after midnight Diana, Princess of Wales left the Ritz Hotel in Paris and got into a waiting Mercedes with her companion Dodi Al Fayed. Speeding off into the night to escape waiting reporters the car crashed at high speed in the Place de L'Alma road tunnel. The driver and Dodi died instantly, but the emergency services arrived to find Diana alive, although seriously injured.

At the nearby Pitie Salpetriere Hospital a team of doctors did all they could, but to no avail, and the Princess, who should, if Fairy Tales are to be believed, have lived happily ever after, died at the tragically young age of thirty-six, at four am, Paris time.

As the people of Britain awoke to hear the terrible news in the early morning bulletins, the sense of loss was palpable across the nation, and within hours, floral tributes began to appear at the gates of Kensington Palace, creating a carpet of colour, the like of which had never been seen before.

The one question upon everyone's lips was quite simply, how could this have happened? Even though Diana had been divorced from the Prince of Wales for the past year and had relinquished her HRH status, she was still officially a member of the Royal family as the mother of the second and third in line to the throne. For the great British public Diana was as much England's rose as she had ever been, and with her increased charity work, remained one of the most popular of all the Royals.

Almost instantly the conspiracy theories began to take flight, and PR for the House of Windsor hit an all-time low, when the beautiful young woman, tipped to lead the Royal family into the 21st Century, was instead laid to rest in the grounds of her ancestral home, Althorp in Northamptonshire.

Diana's death without doubt marked the closing of an extraordinary chapter in the history of the Royal family, but as the years have passed, rather than fading, her memory has lived on to inspire each new generation.

Yet to this day there are still many questions surrounding the death of Diana, Princess of Wales, and chances are no one will ever know for sure the exact chain of events that led to the moment when Diana's life came to such an untimely end. Even so, nothing can detract from the impact Diana had on those who knew her personally, and the rest of us, who watched her progress from afar. And as we remember the Princess who meant such a great deal to so many, we'll follow Diana, from her birth on the Royal Estate at Sandringham in Norfolk, to catch a glimpse of the real-life daughter, wife, mother and Princess, upon whom fate bestowed the fame and fortune mere mortals can only dream of, while dealing her the cruelest of blows.

When Noel Coward observed *"Very flat, Norfolk"*, there's no disputing the fact, but to dismiss this ancient county as a result would be to do it a great injustice. With a stunningly beautiful coastline, quaint market towns, richly verdant agricultural land and the navigable rivers and lakes known as the Broads, this is rural England at its loveliest, and it is the landscape of Princess Diana's birth and childhood.

Sandringham, where Diana was born, is a popular Royal retreat, and as her father, who was destined to become Earl Spencer, was Equerry first to King George VI and then to Diana's future mother-in-law, the Queen, the Spencer family lived at Park House on the magnificent Sandringham estate.

Queen Victoria purchased Sandringham Hall, as it was then known, for her eldest son Bertie, the Prince of Wales and future King Edward VII, for his new bride, Princess Alexandra. When the renovations were complete in 1870 the house was way ahead of its time with gas lighting, flushing toilets and even a very early shower.

Today Sandringham has been the private home of four generations of sovereigns, with the Queen generally in residence over the Christmas holiday until the middle of February. The delightful church of St Mary Magdalene, where Diana was christened, is the focus of much attention on Christmas morning as it's where the Royal family worship, bringing out quite a crowd to witness the festive occasion.

So when The Honorable Diana Frances Spencer was born at Park House, Sandringham on the 1st of July 1961, the fourth child of

Viscount and Viscountess Althorp, she could not have had a better placed arrival for a future Princess.

With two older sisters, Sarah, born in 1955 and Jane, born in 1957, when Diana appeared on the scene the Althorps would have still been hankering after a son and heir, especially as in 1960 their third child, a boy, John, died within hours of his birth. The present Earl Spencer, Charles, Diana's younger brother, was born in 1964, to finally complete the next generation of this aristocratic family.

For onlookers, it would appear that Diana was the most fortunate of children, just as she would be perceived as extremely privileged for the entire duration of her tragically short life.

But things were never as rosy as they seemed. Despite enjoying the delights of 200,000 acres of beautiful Norfolk countryside, which on occasion meant going to tea with the Royal neighbors at the big house, life for the young Spencers was about to be thrown into turmoil.

Diana's father was content living as a gentleman farmer and being part of the community, even playing for the local cricket team, but fourteen years his junior, her mother, after giving birth to five children before she was thirty, longed for the excitement and glamour of London society. Diana was just six when her parents separated after the Viscountess fell in love with Peter Shand Kydd and left her husband. The acrimonious divorce that followed resulted in custody being granted to the Viscount, and consequently Diana had little contact with her mother.

Although close to her father, who she undoubtedly adored, the day-to-day care of the children fell to a succession of nannies, which was far from ideal for the sensitive Diana, who quickly had to learn the art of self-reliance.

The older Spencer girls did well at school, but Diana was far more artistic than academic, and she struggled to keep up with the high standards set by Sarah and Jane. Diana's confidence was further dented when she broke her arm in a riding accident and unlike many of her far from academic peers, she wasn't even able to find solace in ponies and horses.

After attending Silfield School in nearby King's Lynn as a day pupil, Diana followed her sisters to boarding school at the age of nine.

A shy child, Diana was most remembered for her kindness to her fellow pupils, especially those younger than herself, as she grew into her teens. But the Spencer girls faced quite a shock when they returned to Park House for the holidays. In the early 1970s their father brought the new woman in his life to meet his children, Raine, Countess of Dartmouth, the daughter of romantic novelist Barbara Cartland. If Johnny Spencer had hoped to create a "happy" new family he was sadly disappointed, as to say that his children didn't take to Raine as a prospective stepmother, would be a colossal understatement.

This bombshell for the Spencer children was then followed by yet another dramatic change in 1975 when the seventh Earl Spencer, Diana's grandfather, died at the age of 83. Johnny became the eighth Earl Spencer, Charles his son was now Viscount Althorp and Diana, like her sisters, exchanged her "Honorable" title for that of a "Lady". The family moved from Sandringham to the ancestral home at Althorp, complete with 8,500 acres in Northamptonshire.

For the painfully shy Diana, away at boarding school for most of the time, it meant she knew no one in the vicinity, and matters got worse a year later when her father married Raine in July 1976.

Like many great ancestral estates in the 1970s, Althorp needed total renovation and the Spencer children believed that Raine was dominating the proceedings, selling off many of the family treasures to fund the refurbishments, which caused considerable resentment.

These were crucial years for Diana to be experiencing such upheaval and her schoolwork undoubtedly suffered as a result. When she failed to gain academic qualifications, and a finishing school in Switzerland simply left her home sick and unhappy, she headed for London, in search of work.

There were plenty of well to do young families in London, in search of suitable "nannies" for their children, and as caring for little ones made Diana happy, which in turn meant that she was very good at it, she soon carved out a new existence for herself, although she was hardly more than a child herself. In 1978 on the advice of her mother, Diana bought a three bedroomed apartment in Coleherne Court, Fulham, and promptly invited a select group of girls, who were old friends, to house share.

These were blissfully happy days for Diana, and although still painfully shy, she started to meet people her own age and enjoy the young, affluent London scene. After a while she went to work at the Young England Kindergarten in Pimlico, which she described as her first "proper" job, and again Diana excelled, with her young charges adoring her. At last the girl who had craved nothing more in her life than approval and affection had found fulfilment, looking after other people's children.

The late 1970s and early 1980s were exciting times for this new generation of the aristocracy. Benefiting from family money to back them and a London base for Monday to Friday, with a place in the country for weekends, the "Henrys" and "Henriettas" of the landed gentry made the Knightsbridge, South Kensington and Chelsea districts of London their own.

Here, amongst their own kind, with the system of Debutants "out" to do the season now defunct, it was possible for these young people to meet suitable marriage partners, and although times were beginning to change, the main goal of an aristocratic girl was still to marry well and produce the next generation of "Henrys" and "Henriettas".

This part of London, which incorporated Sloane Street and Sloane Square, resulted in this affluent group being dubbed "Sloane Rangers", and to this day a visit to Knightsbridge or South Kensington, will bring you into contact with 21st Century "Sloane Rangers", keeping up the tradition.

That Diana and her flat mates were "Sloanes" is without question, however the future Princess of Wales soon developed a style all her own. With a tall willowy grace, the fair complexion of a classic English rose and an endearingly naïve and innocent charm, even while still in her teens, this was one "Lady" in waiting, who was poised to stand out from the crowd.

When Diana was born, her future husband was just a matter of months away from becoming a teenager, and as we've already established, the pair were destined to move in the same circles. However, if Diana's privileged childhood is considered to have been rather lonely and isolated, the early life of Prince Charles can only be sympathetically regarded in the same light.

On the 14th of November 1948 a baby boy was born at Buckingham Palace to the then Princess Elizabeth, Duchess of Edinburgh and her husband Prince Philip, the Duke of Edinburgh. Christened Charles Philip Arthur George, the Prince was their first child and had the succession run unhindered after the death of King George V in 1936, the solemn prospect of becoming a King may never have fallen upon the child's shoulders.

By rights the first son of King George V, Edward VIII should have remained on the British throne until his death in 1972, but his determination to marry the divorcee Wallis Simpson, the woman he loved, resulted in his abdication.

Therefore, the next in line, George the fifth's second son, the Duke of York stepped unexpectedly into the limelight, to become King George the sixth. With Queen Elizabeth, his wife, and two young daughters at his side, despite his shyness and a nervous stammer, George VI became a much loved and respected sovereign. In a difficult age, as Britain faced the horrors of World War II, the King shared the experience of his people, as London burned, and even worked with determination to overcome his stammer, in order to boost public morale. On the balcony of Buckingham Palace, he celebrated VE Day with all of London in 1945, and in the post-war era continued to restore the reputation of the monarchy, after the constitutional crisis brought about by his brother's abdication.

That George VI rose to the challenges that fate had thrust upon him is without question, but it wasn't only his personal circumstances that changed. Elizabeth, his eldest daughter also faced the same constitutional duties asked of her father, but as the Heiress Presumptive she was given more time than George VI to prepare for the Royal role of sovereign. On her 21st birthday, she declared that her whole life would be devoted to the service of her people, and it was a promise that the young Princess took very seriously indeed.

When Princess Elizabeth married Prince Philip, a member of the Greek Royal family and a second cousin, once removed, it was exactly as protocol would have dictated, although it's been suggested that the Princess fell in love with her handsome Prince while still a girl in her teens.

After the arrival of Charles in 1948, Princess Anne was born in 1950, and despite the expectation that Charles would one day become King, it was still a long way off. Nevertheless, when his grandfather's health began to falter in 1951, his mother's accession to the throne was becoming more imminent than anyone realized. George VI died at Sandringham House on the 6th of February 1952 at the age of 56, and a few months shy of her 26th birthday the new Queen, Elizabether II was called upon to do her constitutional duty, at a time of great personal loss, still grieving for her father.

So it was that His Royal Highness Prince Charles, aged just three, became Duke of Cornwall, Duke of Rothesay, Earl of Carrick and Baron Renfrew, Lord of the Isles, Prince and Great Steward of Scotland, and if that wasn't enough for a toddler to cope with, he also became the Heir Apparent.

Now, should you be wondering what the difference is between an Heir Apparent and an Heir Presumptive, it's quite simple. Prince Charles as Heir Apparent cannot be removed from his position as first in line to the throne. Technically when George VI became King, if he had gone on to produce a male heir, his eldest daughter, now Queen Elizabeth II, as Heiress Presumptive, would have had to give precedence to a younger sibling because he was a boy.

With his mother now occupied with matters of state and his father often away for significant periods of time because of his Naval duties, just as had been the case for Diana, the day-to-day care of Charles fell to nannies and other members of the Royal family, most notably his beloved Grandmother, Queen Elizabeth, the Queen Mother. His circumstances were very different to Diana's, but the need for parental attention, approval and affection would have been just the same, no matter how grand the palaces were that he happened to be living in.

It's been said on numerous occasions throughout history that with great wealth and power comes great responsibility, the ancient tradition of "Noblesse Oblige", and for Charles, service, duty and the path to Kingship probably dominated his childhood, and for that matter, his entire adult life.

Charles was created Prince of Wales in 1958, in keeping with the historic precedent of the reigning monarch bestowing the title upon the Heir Apparent, since Edward I did, way back in 1301.

Ironically through the pages of the history books the title of Prince of Wales does not guarantee accession to the throne and since the first investiture of Edward II, seven have so far failed to go on to become King. Also, the high-profile role of the Princess of Wales, the wife of the prince, has been graced by a number of fascinating women, not least Diana, Princess of Wales, the most famous of them all.

Breaking with the tradition of future monarchs being educated in isolation by tutors, Prince Charles was sent to school from the age of eight, firstly in London, then Kent, and Scotland. Equally as sensitive as Diana was, Charles is reported to have found boarding at Gordonstoun School in Scotland difficult, miles from home in austere surroundings, where his father, the Duke of Edinburgh, had thrived.

Charles completed his education at Gordonstoun, including two terms at Geelong Grammar School in Australia, leaving with good qualifications including A Levels in History and French. Rather than going straight into the military, as was traditional for the Heir Apparent, Charles went to Trinity College, Cambridge as an undergraduate, reading Anthropology, Archaeology and History. When he graduated with a BA in 1970, he actually made history, as the first member of the Royal Family to earn a degree.

Now considered the most eligible young man in Britain, if not perhaps the whole world, public, and therefore press interest, was already fuelling speculation about a suitable match for the prince.

In 1969 Charles's investiture as Prince of Wales was held at Caernarvon Castle, another historic first, as the ceremony was held in Wales, and as the event was televised, millions tuned in to watch the Queen bestow this honor on her eldest son.

It was in the same year that the Queen took the decision to allow the BBC to film a documentary about the personal lives of herself and the Royal family, including her two younger sons Prince Andrew and Prince Edward, born in 1960 and 1964. The program proved very popular with the public and was a dignified response to the growing media demands faced by the monarchy, nevertheless it heralded a new and dangerous era that would culminate in the tragic death of Diana, Princess of Wales, before the end of the century.

When Prince Charles embarked upon a Naval career in 1971, complete with dashing uniform, press interest in any girl he so much as developed a friendship with escalated. As a future King, he would be expected to produce heirs of his own, and the hunt was on for a suitable bride for the sailor Prince.

On paper finding such a lady was quite a tall order, especially at a time when young women, whether high born or commoners, were enjoying greater independence and sexual freedom than ever before.

It was required that a prospective Princess of Wales, and future Queen, should be protestant, not a divorcee, meet the approval of her future Mother-in-Law, Elizabeth II, and ideally be a virgin, with aristocratic connections and no colorful past for the press to delve into.

Many of the young ladies with whom Charles had been linked failed to meet these exacting requirements, but interestingly when he dated Lady Sarah Spencer, Diana's older sister, in the late 1970s a Royal Wedding looked to be on the cards. However, despite Lady Sarah's eminent suitability a marriage proposal was not forthcoming, and the couple parted company, but not before Charles had come into contact with the incredibly shy but blossoming Lady Diana Spencer. History, as they say, was in the making.

Ever since the 'swingin' sixties', London had become an exciting, vibrant and fashionable place to be, and as the equally colorful seventies ended, it appeared that Prince Charles was settling rather comfortably into bachelordom, then a tragedy occurred that quite literally turned his world upside down.

When the Provisional IRA murdered Earl Mountbatter of Burma in a bomb blast, while he was out sailing in Donegal Bay on 27th August 1979, they committed a terrorist atrocity that not only shocked the world, but also robbed Prince Charles of a much-loved Great Uncle, who happened to be, in all probability, the single most significant male in his life. It's been said that the pair referred to each other as "Honorary Grandfather" and "Honorary Grandson", and the younger man always listened to what his worldly-wise relation had to say.

Great Uncle Louis had without doubt lived life to the full, with a glamorous circle of acquaintance including Royalty and the new generation of celebrities from the Hollywood film industry, counting such luminaries as Charlie Chaplin, Douglas Fairbanks and Mary Pickford amongst his closest friends.

Having watched the previous Prince of Wales, Edward VIII, abdicate over a woman, while being no stranger to the gossip columnists himself over the years, he is reputed to have advised Prince Charles to enjoy the bachelor life while he could, and then marry a young, pure, inexperienced girl to ensure the succession.

As Prince Charles grieved for Mountbatten he turned to an old friend, Camilla Parker Bowles for support, facing also the recognition of his own mortality. Naturally, he wanted to honour the

Earl's memory, and it appears he was now ready to settle down and find a Princess of Wales to stand beside him, as he prepared to face up to the responsibilities of being Heir Apparent.

With the benefit of hindsight, if he could have married Camilla at that time, then the tragedy of Diana's death could have been averted, but she was already married, and as we already know, even if she had divorced her husband, the threat to the constitutional monarchy, such a relatively short time after the abdication of Edward VIII, would have been disastrous.

In such an impossible situation, Camilla, as the prince's friend, joined the search for a suitable bride. As the 70s gave way to the 80s, all eyes turned towards London, and more specifically Coleherne Court, home to a group of girls about town, one of whom was of course, Lady Diana Spencer.

At 19, Diana who had watched the prince from close quarters at Sandringham, was not surprisingly swept off her feet by the attentions of a sophisticated, charming, older man. Diana was invited to join the circle of acquaintance she had always been on the edge of, including parties on HMS Britannia, the Royal Yacht, during Cowes week on the Isle of Wight. Today this beautiful craft is no longer in service, and can be found at Leith, the Port of Edinburgh, where it is a very popular attraction. However, even at a distance so many years later, it's easy to see how a tender-hearted young woman, with little life experience, looking for romance, would have fallen in love with the prince who opened up such an exciting and glamorous new world to her.

Back in London a relationship between Charles and Diana flourished, with romantic, candle-lit dinners at Buckingham Palace, supposedly in secret. But it wasn't long before the world's press set up camp outside Coleherne Court and the Young England Kindergarten where Diana worked.

Lady Diana Spencer was demure and charming despite the harassment, proving herself suitably discreet, and with this test passed, she was whisked off to see how she would cope in Scotland, watching the prince and his friends fishing and shooting, as all the while Diana continued to stake her claim to the title, Princess of Wales.

Diana was also introduced to the county of Gloucestershire, often dubbed the Royal County, because of the number of Royals with country residences there. Charles took Diana to visit Highgrove, the country house he bought early in 1980, close to the delightful market town of Tetbury. It was during one of the Gloucestershire weekends that Charles took Diana to meet Camilla, and with his friend's approval, broached the subject of marriage.

The official engagement between Prince Charles and Lady Diana Spencer was announced by Buckingham Palace on the 24th of February 1981. In the photographs to mark the occasion, the bride to be wore a blue outfit from Harrods, and it was evident for all to see that she adored her fiancée.

It was no longer practical for the future Princess of Wales to flat share in Fulham, and immediately after the engagement was announced she moved into Clarence House, the home of the Prince's Grandmother, the Queen Mother.

In the months leading up to the Royal Wedding in July, Lady Di fever swept the land. As she asked advice from Vogue, where her sister Jane worked, Diana developed a style that was extremely feminine with pie frill collars, pussy cat bows and long, floral skirts, which the High Street fashion stores were quick to emulate. Hairdressers up and down the land were asked to reproduce Diana's long, blonde, flicked fringe, and the demand for nannies who were aristocratic young English girls skyrocketed.

Although Royal Weddings usually favored Westminster Abbey, St Paul's Cathedral was the chosen venue, accommodating the unprecedented 3,500 guests. It was a fairy tale ending to a modern-day love story, and when the newlyweds set off for Broadlands, Hampshire, the home of Earl Mountbatten, for the first night of their honeymoon, before taking a Mediterranean Cruise aboard the Royal Yacht Britannia, the whole world wished them well, and expected them to live happily ever after.

And for a while, the Prince and Princess of Wales looked to have found the love and security they both so desperately needed, with each other. If the public at large needed further confirmation, an announcement from Buckingham Palace revealing that the Princess was pregnant, three months after returning from honeymoon, ensured that the next generation of Royals became more popular than ever.

When Diana gave birth to a baby boy, at St Mary's Hospital, London, on the 21st June 1982, no one could have asked more of her, and her son, styled, His Royal Highness Prince William of Wales immediately took his place as second in line to the throne.

A further visit to St Mary's for the birth of HRH Henry of Wales, better known to the world as Harry, on the 15th of September 1984, made the future of the constitutional monarchy even more secure. It's been suggested that Prince Charles had hoped for a daughter, but a healthy son, third in line to the throne, was again, all anyone could have reasonably asked of the Princess of Wales.

That Diana, Princess of Wales adored her two sons is beyond question, but as she fulfilled her Royal duties, whether based at her London home, Kensington Palace or Highgrove in Gloucestershire, the strain was beginning to show. By the mid-eighties there was already speculation that all was not well, behind these fine gates, between the Prince and his Fairy Tale Princess, not helped by the glamorous sense of style Diana had developed, as she grew into one of the world's most beautiful women.

Wherever the Prince and Princess of Wales went, at home or abroad, the crowds who flocked to see them were invariably more interested in what the Princess was wearing, rather than what the more serious-minded Prince had to say. However, Diana paid a high price for her status as a fashion icon, suffering from an eating disorder that was most probably Bulimia Nervosa.

In just a few short years the beautiful English rose who had promised to breathe new life into the Royal Family, had been stifled by duty and protocol, and Charles, who had always tried to follow the motto of every Prince of Wales, "Ich Dien", meaning "I Serve", found himself right back where he had started, before Diana had agreed to marry him.

What happened next is well documented through newspaper and television archives, as Charles once more turned to Camilla Parker Bowles for comfort, and Diana searched for solace in what she thought to be a discreet affair.

As head of the Royal family, the Queen faced a constitutional crisis every bit as explosive as the abdication of Edward VIII, which resulted in her father becoming King back in the 1930s. Matters deteriorated further and by 1992, after the break down of her daughter Princess Anne's marriage and the separation of her second son Prince Andrew from his wife, Sarah, Duchess of York, the Queen described this as an Annus Horribilis, which translates from the Latin as quite simply a horrible year. Added to so much family turmoil, Windsor Castle, the place the Queen regards as her true home, was damaged by fire and before the year was out the Prince and Princess of Wales had also separated.

As the world's press looked on Diana continued to live at Kensington Palace, enjoying time there with her "boys". Charles spent a lot of time at Highgrove in Gloucestershire, where the young Princes had plenty of opportunity to make the most of the beautiful countryside, while they were with their father. Just as is the case for all families that face a marital split, these were difficult times, and for the Prince and Princess of Wales, struggling to find resolution for the sake of the children, the constant press attention did nothing to make things any easier.

However, despite her troubled personal circumstances Diana continued to work tirelessly for charity, campaigning to improve public perception of AIDS sufferers and highlight the terrible destruction caused by landmines, as she fought for a worldwide ban on these cruelly devastating weapons of war.

Ironically, this undoubtedly worthy, high-profile stance of the Princess caused the Royal family some difficulty, especially when Diana hit the headlines as she attempted to carve out a new life for herself. It was now extremely unlikely that Diana could still become Queen, but it wasn't conclusively resolved, and the public adoration that she generated continued undiminished, and Prince Charles as the nation's future King was forever going to find himself overshadowed by Diana. Eventually the couple's divorce was finalized in 1996, a year and three days before Diana's death on the streets of Paris.

And so, we return to where we began this remembrance of Diana, with the whole world in shock at the loss of this truly remarkable young woman.

On a fine September morning, London basking in early autumn sunlight, prepared to bid Diana a final farewell.

Her funeral was held at Westminster Abbey at 11.00am on Saturday the 6th of September 1997. The Royal family were all in attendance alongside the Spencers, led by Diana's younger brother Charles, now the Earl. As was only right and proper, the main focus was to support Diana's two sons, William and Harry, so despite conspiracy theories abounding and an element of antagonism levelled at both the press and the Royal family, the funeral of Diana, Princess of Wales was as dignified as it was moving.

After the service, watched by millions around the world, Diana's mortal remains were carried on an incredible journey home, to Althorp in Northamptonshire. All the way from London's familiar landmarks, northwards, the funeral cortege was greeted by literally thousands of ordinary folks, waiting to pay their last respects to the People's Princess.

Even along the verges of the M1 motorway entire families joined together to say their fond farewells, and by the time Diana eventually reached the gates of Althorp for the last time, the cortege was more than an hour late.

Understandably Diana's family wanted to bury her where she could no longer be subject to press intrusion, and her grave couldn't be more private, on an island in the middle of the Oval Lake in the grounds of Althorp. In the years since, those closest to Diana have been able to visit her grave in absolute privacy, which as her sons face the full glare of publicity that dominated Diana's adult life, no doubt they have very much appreciated this.

Nevertheless, it has been difficult for the millions of people who would have also liked to commemorate the anniversaries of Diana's life and death, with nowhere specific to gather. The gates at Kensington Palace where so many floral tributes appeared way back in 1997 will often be where people choose to place flowers. But a memorial in one of the great churches like Westminster Abbey, where her funeral took place, or St Paul's Cathedral, where she married, would certainly prove popular with visitors who wish to remember Diana with thoughtful contemplation, and as her memory lives on, who can say what the future might bring.

However, for many people a tour around the country to quietly walk in the footsteps of this unforgettable Princess, will always be a very special and rewarding experience.

From the magnificent Sandringham Estate in Norfolk to the beautiful Althorp House in Northamptonshire, these great Stately Homes so much a part of the nation's heritage, have times when they are open to the public. Also, a visit to Gloucestershire will prove very interesting. Despite Highgrove, the home of Prince Charles not being open to the public, the delightful, neighbouring market town of Tetbury is fascinating, especially when you count the number of "By Royal Appointment" signs over the shops. And of course, those of us with an interest in Diana, enjoy following the progress of her two sons, Prince William and Prince Harry, so what could be nicer than savoring a pint of finest English Ale where the princes have been known to partake of the hospitality when they're staying at Highgrove?

Everywhere Diana went, she touched the lives of those she met, bringing joy and hope to where it was most needed, but if you really want to experience the true spirit of this elusive butterfly, then London is the place to go.

Beginning with Buckingham Palace, you can walk down the Mall following the route Diana took to St Paul's Cathedral on that eventful July morning, leaving the palace as Lady Diana Spencer, to return as the Princess of Wales, and future Queen.

As a point of interest, the Spencer family name is attached to the magnificent Spencer House, which offers guided tours on the Sundays it's open to the public.

When the first Earl Spencer was a prominently society figure back in the 18th Century, this neo-classical treasure put him at the heart of London, literally just across Green Park from Buckingham Palace. Although hundreds of years later Lady Diana Spencer lived in a modern flat very different to the grand facade of the town house; Spencer House is nonetheless a timely reminder of Diana's impeccable ancestry, in her own right.

By contrast a trip to Coleherne Court will always raise a smile, remembering the vibrancy of Diana as a blossoming bride-to-be, courted by her Fairy Tale Prince. And naturally a visit to Harrods is an absolute must. Here you will find the stylish designers that Diana adored as a girl about town, but much, much more. There is a permanent memorial to Diana, Princess of Wales and Dodi Al Fayed, put in place by the historic store's owner, Mohamed Al Fayed, the father of Diana's companion who died with her on that fateful night in Paris.

The official Princess of Wales Memorial Fountain in Hyde Park was opened by the Queen in 2004, to symbolise Diana's great affinity and openness with people from all walks of life. However, the Fountain has not been without its critics, and many feel a memorial close to Diana's Kensington Palace home, far more appropriate. Kensington Gardens have always been associated with Peter Pan, as it's where the author JM Barrie met the little boys who inspired him to write his masterpiece.

Here the Diana, Princess of Wales Memorial Playground recreates the world of Peter Pan and is a fitting tribute to a Princess who had such a special way with children.

As our journal draws to a close, this is perhaps the perfect place to remember Diana, Princess of Wales. For an all too short period of history she lit up the world, and shone so bright that her legacy, as you've read for yourself, lives on. And perhaps the most precious gift bequeathed by Diana to the nation are her sons, Prince William and Prince Harry. Diana's determination to help them lead happy, fulfilled lives, knowing that their parents loved them, is a lasting testament to an English rose that will blossom eternally.

Yet the story of Diana, Princess of Wales only goes to show that there's no predicting what the future might hold for any of us, and although we will always feel sadness for a life lost so tragically young, Diana will forever be remembered, where it matters most, in the hearts of those for whom she would have been proud to be Queen.

FOOTNOTES:
I have three personal experience links with Diana. The earliest, is down to confidential pillow chat with a very high society lady I had a relationship with and therefore cannot reveal. The lady was in fact a roommate of Diana at boarding school back in the day. After lights out one night, when girls would chat about their future dreams, plans and wishes, amongst a plethora of socialites, nurses, doctors and show jumpers, Diana quietly pipped in saying, "I'm going to be the Princess of Wales". After a moment of silence there followed jolly banter and teasing.

Diana was 12 years old.

The next experience is media related. I was featured in that classiest of UK tabloids "The Sun" in 1990, a virtually double page article. Sales were hugely boosted that day with a frontpage picture of Diana giving the young William a slap for pushing the royal behavior too far. I was grateful for the boost the outrage gave to MY article that day.

Even more so seven years later, when the opening prog of my then new Prime time BBC series had a four centre pages spread in the Sunday Express Magazine. The same week as Diana's funeral. The Sunday Express wrapped that week's issue in a special "keep sake/souvenir" wrap around. And printed not their usual 250,000 copies, which would have served well as series publicity. Instead, they printed 1.5 million copies. I was again an unexpected publicity beneficiary as a result of far more tragic Diana story.

Lastly, WHERE is Diana truly laid to rest?

When I was flying over Althorp Park in 2007, to get aerial footage for a Diana documentary, the local helicopter pilot informed me that Diana was NOT buried on the Althorp Island as publicly stated.

Rather, she had been "secretly interned" at the family crypt in the local church during the hours of darkness, confirmed by witnesses to the night-time disturbances. Followed up by a report of fresh, wet mortar on the tomb itself the following day.

The ploy of advising the public that her remains were ensconced on the island inside the estate; an attempt to reduce pressure on the church itself as a shrine for visiting loyalist and Diana followers. OR as some would have it, a steering of income by visitors directly TO Althorp Park.

Yet another conspiracy theory? Who knows, but I find helicopter pilots, intelligent and usually reliable sources of information. We "buzzed" Althorp for just a few minutes as the occupants tend to complain at aerial intrusion. As well as ground-based incursions. Therefore, I will not be visiting with a spade.

LIAM DALE

❖ ❖ ❖

ROYAL HERITAGE

AUTHOR NOTE:

Based on a History Journal one hour read, Royal Heritage covers a fair bit of previous chapters. However, I thought it a useful "bonus" at the end of this Royal Collection, rather than leave it out. You might pick up some details not previously covered. It does however create a "revisionary reminder" of British Royal History, offering text cut n copy for academic students.

****

Anybody who visits London at the height of the summer will soon realize that the United Kingdom's capital city attracts sightseers from every far-flung corner of the globe. And what's on their list of attractions to see? Nine times out of ten it will be Buckingham Palace, often followed by the Tower of London, and since the tragic death of Diana, Princess of Wales in 1997, her former residence, Kensington Palace.

In an age when the monarchy, British or otherwise, is accused of being an outdated institution, the tourists still flock in their millions to follow in the footsteps of Royalty, both ancient and modern, to see for themselves the places where history was made.

When it comes to listing the great Kings and Queens of the past, there are undoubtedly some that are better remembered than others. Richard the Lion Heart, Henry the Eighth and King George the third are renowned for very different reasons and when it comes to the ladies, Mary the first, both of them, one of England and one of Scotland, Elizabeth the first and Queen Victoria are as fascinating today as when they were alive.

But there are many more characters worthy of investigation that are far less well known. So, whether you want a basic who's, who of the British Monarchy to help you in the next pub quiz, or you'd like to find out how we got from feuding tribes of Ancient Britons to the present day, prepare for a right Royal romp through the history books so that you never need to get your Henrys, Georges, Edwards, Richards, Marys and Williams mixed up again!

Before we get down to the nitty gritty of succession, it's well worth stepping back further in time to take a closer look at the British Isles just after the birth of Christ, when the Romans were masters of all they surveyed, including a large part of the United Kingdom. Of the native Brits, many of whom were Celts, there was considerable opposition to the Roman occupation, not least from the woman often dubbed the Queen of the Ancient Britons, Boudicca, or if you happen to be of a certain age, Boadicea.

This fearsome warrior Queen led her Iceni tribe to revolt against the Romans, and as neighbouring tribes of Ancient Britons swelled their numbers, Boudicca led a campaign that advanced from Colchester all the way to London and beyond, until the Romans finally managed to stop her in her tracks.

Without actual records it is hard to be precise about dates, it's believed Boudicca came to prominence in about AD 61, but even after her death the Romans continued to have problems with the Celts. Rather than face the Scots in the North, who were as fearsome as the great warrior Queen, in AD 122, the Roman Emperor Hadrian built a wall to keep the Scots out of England. This early separation of the neighboring nations would continue for centuries, but more on that subject later!

Eventually the Roman Occupation came to an end when the overstretched Empire recalled their soldiers back to Rome but waiting in the wings were the bloodthirsty Saxons ready with invasion plans of their own.

However, if legend is to be believed one man united the tribes of the British Isles to resist the Saxon advances, and it is quite possible that he came from Wales. We have all heard of King Arthur and his Knights of the Round Table, fighting for chivalry and honour in a lawless age, but try and find him in an historic timeline, and you really will struggle.

A true Celt, Arthur is thought to have lived in the 5th Century AD, and this immediately gives us a major problem, historically. Our images of King Arthur and his gallant Knights belong to a much later age, but there is a very good reason for this.

Way back in the 12th Century, a bishop known as Geoffrey of Monmouth wrote a "History of the Kings of Britain" and where the facts were a little sketchy, he simply filled in the blanks. Consequently, Geoffrey's rendition of the King Arthur story was set in the time that he knew best, his own, and we have had Knights in shining armour and damsels in distress ever since.

Fascinating as this may, or may not be, it just goes to prove that we need to view history books with care, and especially when it comes to Royalty, because what may appear as fact, might well, indeed, merely be fiction.

Therefore, with images of King Arthur's mortal remains sailing away with the Lady of the Lake, and his sword Excalibur disappearing beneath the waters of Dozmary Pool, we will move onto a time when history is far more reliably documented.

After the demise of Arthur, the Saxon occupiers in waiting, invaded, and by 613 had driven the Celts out of England.

Seven Kingdoms were then established: Kent, Sussex, Essex, East Anglia, Wessex, Mercia, and Northumbria, with each having its own King. Eventually one of the Kings, Egbert of Wessex took control of all Seven Kingdoms after much fighting, to be the first

King of England in 829, with his son and grandsons succeeding him. In fact, one of the earliest Kings most of us will have heard of was Alfred the Great, and he was a grandson of Egbert, but in popular culture is much better remembered for being a very bad cook!

Alfred became King of England in 871, and by all accounts, was a well educated man who as a child had been taken to visit the Pope in Rome, not an inconsiderable achievement in the 9th Century. However, England was once more under threat of invasion, this time by the Danes, and this is how the story of the burnt cakes came about. Alfred escaped an attack by the Danes in the West Country and legend has it that he sought refuge with peasants living on the Somerset levels, while he contemplated how to save his Kingdom.

One day when the peasant's wife went out on errands, Alfred was left in charge of her baking, but he was so caught up with matters of state, he forgot all about the cooking and was duly chastised when the woman returned to burnt cakes.

Whether true or not, this is the story that has gone down in the history books, when Alfred was in fact, as his name suggests, a much greater King than this footnote gives him credit for.

After Alfred and a succession of Ed's of all varieties, including an Elder, a Fair and a Martyr, the next King that most of us will have heard of is Ethelred the Unready, who came to the throne in 978.

However, it is a case of meaning being lost in translation, because "Unraed", what he was actually called, means "poorly counselled" in Anglo-Saxon, and the unfortunate Ethelred might have benefited from some good advice. The Danes were still on the rampage and Ethelred was no match for the Viking leader Sweyn Forkbeard, who seized the English throne in 1013. But Forkbeard's reign was short lived, as he died about five weeks later, and despite his wonderful name referring to the way he wore his beard, it's his son Canute who is much better remembered, and all because of another much-loved Royal legend.

King Canute ruled England from 1016, after a brief reversion to Ethelred's son, and he was one of the best monarchs the country had ever known. Wise and fair, Canute modernised the laws of the land, although many believe he considered himself so important he attempted to command the seas and the turn of the tide. However, this could not be further from the truth. Tired of his courtier's flattery, when one insisted Canute could order the tide not to come in, Canute went down to the beach, set up his throne at the water's edge and of course got wet, proving that he had no power over the elements, while at the same time exposing the courtier as very foolish indeed!

When Canute died, he was succeeded firstly by his son Harold and then his other son, Harthacanute. When he died the throne passed again back to the Saxon line and another son of Ethelred the Unready, who was also the half-brother of Harthacanute, known as Edward the Confessor, a title which was bestowed upon him because of his great piety.

Nevertheless, Edward failed to produce a son and heir, and this caused a real problem, especially as it seems he promised the English throne to both his brother-in-law, Harold Godwinson and his distant cousin, William, Duke of Normandy.

Edward the Confessor died in 1066, a year familiar to us all because of the Battle of Hastings. When Harold became King, Cousin William over in France was not content to give up his claim to the English throne. William was also a descendent of Alfred the Great, and when he set out to conquer England, there was no stopping him. Harold was killed in the Battle of Hastings, depicted in the Bayeux Tapestry as being shot by an arrow through the eye, and the event heralded the Norman period of English history, quite literally changing the face of the nation during William's well-documented Norman Conquests.

When William was crowned King at the newly constructed Westminster Abbey, on Christmas Day 1066, he was ready to take control of the nation. Anglo-Saxon estates were confiscated and granted to Norman nobles, and needless to say the natives got very restless. William and his nobles put down many revolts, building their characteristic castles and fortresses all over the land, including the original White Tower of the Tower of London, constructed in 1078. And to ensure his supremacy, William is also remembered for the compilation of the Domesday Book in 1085, an early form of census that recorded how land was being used, and more importantly for the Norman Treasury, how much tax could be levied on the people of England.

Not that William lived long enough to personally reap the benefits as he died in 1087 after falling from his horse in France. It is important to remember that these early Kings were military leaders as well as monarchs and with lands in France and England, William certainly had his work cut out.

After William I came his son, William II, known as William Rufus because of his ruddy complexion. He too was kept busy, especially as the Scottish King Malcolm III tried, on more than one occasion, to invade his English neighbour, as did Welsh rebels unhappy with the Norman nobles occupying the boarder castles of the Marches.

William Rufus however was not killed in battle, but in a hunting accident while out with friends in the New Forest, although the conspiracy theorists have a different version of events.

Henry I, William's youngest brother was crowned at Westminster Abbey in 1100 and it has been suggested that he may have had a hand in his brother's untimely death. Henry nonetheless pledged good governance and wisely neutralized any threat from Scotland by marrying the daughter of the troublesome, by now deceased, Malcolm III. But not everything ran to plan; his brother, the Duke of Normandy attempted to overthrow Henry, and the King lost his only son, William, who was drowned at sea.

Now, this is where it gets interesting. Henry 1st had a daughter, Matilda, who as a female was not expected to inherit the throne, but the King persuaded the Barons to accept her as his lawful successor.

This may have been fine in theory, but when Henry died in 1135, Matilda was usurped by her cousin Stephen. Matilda may not have been crowned Queen, but she did not give up her claim to her father's throne without a fight.

These were turbulent years characterized by Civil War, only brought to a satisfactory conclusion when Stephen agreed to name Matilda's son, Henry Plantagenet, Count of Anjou, as his heir. Consequently, when Stephen died in 1154, he was the last Norman King of England, as Henry II became the first of the Plantagenets.

It's obvious the Normans came from Normandy, but if you're wondering where the Plantagenets came from, it's actually all down to a nickname. Geoffrey, Count of Anjou, Henry's father always wore a sprig of flowering Broom, Planta Genista and this is how he was known.

When Henry II was crowned King of England in 1154, aged 21, he was already Count of Anjou and Toraine, as well as being Duke of Normandy and Acquitaine, which meant his French territories were more extensive than those owned by the King of France. Add to that the throne of England, and Henry's Angevin Empire stretched from the Solway Firth to the Pyrenees.

So far, we have focused on the monarchs, and not mentioned their Queens, but in the case of Henry II, his wife, Eleanor of Acquitaine must be one of the most fascinating historical characters of all time.

The pair were married in France in 1152, the bride being eleven years her handsome groom's senior. Eleanor had first been married to the King of France but had been granted an annulment because they were so closely related and when Henry came to the English throne, he brought with him a charismatic Queen, who was centuries ahead of her time.

Just as Alfred's remembered for burning the cakes, there is one incident that is synonymous with Henry II; the bloody murder of Thomas a Becket in Canterbury Cathedral in 1170. As monarch, Henry had been determined to control the power of the church and appointed his friend Becket to the influential post of Archbishop of Canterbury in 1162. But Becket would not be swayed from his religious principles and for eight years thwarted the King's reforms, enraging Henry so much, that on one occasion he screamed out *"Will not someone rid me of this turbulent Priest"*.

Immediately four of Henry's Knights took him at his word and set off for Canterbury, and murdered Becket at the High Alter of the Cathedral. Whether this was the King's intention, or a tragic error, Henry II has gone down in the history books with blood on his hands.

Other notable achievements in Henry's reign included the establishment of trial by jury and the acquisition of the title Lord of all Ireland, to go with all the others, in 1171 after a successful invasion.

However, Henry II did not die a happy man. His constant arguments with his wife resulted in her being confined to the French Castle of Chinon for years, and not surprisingly she sided with her son Richard in battle against her husband.

Neither was his relationship with his sons much better and he refused to name an heir, until his dying breath in 1189, when he bequeathed the Angevin Empire to his third son Richard.

And so we come to one of the best-loved English Kings of all time, Richard the Lionheart, friend of Robin Hood, Crusader Knight and darling of literature. But just as some Kings have been misrepresented as poor monarchs, Richard benefited from an over inflated reputation. Of the ten years Richard ruled, he only spent seven months of that time in England, while he plundered the nation's coffers and increased taxation to pay for his Crusades in the Holy Land. Interestingly it is Richard's younger brother John who generally gets the blame for this heavy taxation, especially in the legends of Robin Hood.

Richard the Lionheart was only forty-one when he died in 1199, shot by an archer in France, while he was in search of buried treasure, and his tomb can be found in Fontevrault Abbey next to those of his father Henry and his mother Eleanor, in the heart of the French countryside.

Like Henry II, Richard named his heir as he was dying, and it was his brother John, who has gone down in history, perhaps unfairly, as being as bad a King as Richard was good. King John's best known for signing the Magna Carta at Runnymede in 1215 to appease the warring Barons, and this historic document was crucial in the establishment of English Common Law.

When John died a year later the English throne passed to his son, crowned King Henry III in 1216, at the age of nine, under a regency. However, when Henry took full control in 1227, he proved to be a most unpopular King, and the Barons quietened by Magna Carta, were soon on the rampage again. It fell to Henry's eldest son Prince Edward to put the rebellion down, which he did with great relish.

When Henry III died in 1272 Edward was on Crusade in the Holy Land but returned to be crowned King in 1274. Edward I is often known by the name Longshanks because he was very tall, and he was also renowned for his savagery towards opponents. The Welsh certainly suffered at his hands when Wales was incorporated into his domain, and he was the first to appoint his eldest son Prince of Wales in 1301, a tradition that continues to this day.

However, he is most famous for his barbaric treatment of the Scots. After deposing the Scottish King in 1296 he stole the Stone of Destiny from Scone Palace, a historic artefact used in the Scot's coronation ceremony, and took it to Westminster Abbey where it remained until its return to Edinburgh Castle in 1996.

Nevertheless, when Edward I invaded Scotland, he did not quite have it all his own way, thanks to the efforts of a now famous Scotsman by the name of William Wallace, whose armies beat the English at Sterling Bridge in 1297.

Edward did defeat the Scots a year later at Falkirk, when Wallace was captured and taken to London, where he was executed, but when Robert the Bruce was crowned King of Scotland in 1306, the oppressed nation North of the border served notice that the English now had a fight on their hands.

Upon the death of Edward I, in 1307, ironically on his way North for another go at invading Scotland, his son Edward II, the first ever Prince of Wales, was crowned king.

The new King did not have the stomach for fighting the Scots, and Robert the Bruce assured Scottish Independence in 1314 when he routed the English at the Battle of Bannockburn.

Yet Edward II's most dangerous adversary proved to his wife Queen Isabella, who ran off with her lover, Roger Mortimer, and the pair seized power in the name of the King's eldest son, again called Edward. Edward II was imprisoned in Berkeley Castle, where he was brutally murdered in 1327 on the orders of Isabella and has gone down in history as one of the most unfortunate Kings of all time.

When Edward III finally seized power from the regency of Roger Mortimer in 1330, his 50-year reign proved him to be an affable King, much loved by his people. However, when he died in 1377, Edward's most notable contribution to the history books was his declaration of himself as heir to the French throne, starting what would become the Hundred Years War.

Sadly though, his eldest son, Edward the Black Prince pre-deceased his father, but having produced a son of his own before his untimely demise, Richard II came to the throne at the age of 10. Many believe Richard to have been a weak King, not least because of the play written by William Shakespeare about him. However, he crossed swords with his cousin Henry Bolinbroke, who deposed Richard in 1399 to become Henry IV, the first King of the House of Lancaster, a branch of the Plantagenets. But his prize proved to be something of a poisoned chalice, with nothing but revolts and treasury shortages, and he died a rather disappointed man in 1413.

Succeeded by his son Henry the fifth, Henry the fourth would no doubt have been extremely proud of his heir. After reviving the 100 Years War with France, his armies were victorious at the Battle of Agincourt, again made famous by one of Shakespeare's plays. As a result, upon his death in 1422, his son Henry VI became King inheriting both the English and French thrones.

Henry VI was a good man, but a weak King and during his reign the English were thrown out of France after a campaign led in the first instance by Joan of Arc. The Plantagenet House of York also went into battle with Henry in the War of the Roses, which broke out in 1455, resulting in the Duke of York, the future Edward IV, deposing Henry in 1461. After much too-ing and fro-ing, Henry VI was restored to the throne, but only for a very short time as he was murdered in the Tower of London, very possibly by the Duke of Gloucester who is also suspected of murdering Henry's son, who by rights would have become King.

Consequently, Edward IV was restored to the English throne in 1471, the first King of the House of York. Despite his interrupted reign, Edward proved to be an able King who brought peace and prosperity to England, however when he fell out with his brother George, the unfortunate sibling was found murdered in the Tower of London, something that was proving to be a regular occurrence.

When Edward IV died in 1483, his young son Edward succeeded him, however the boy's uncle claimed the child illegitimate and seized the throne for himself. The King in question was Richard III and when Edward V and his younger brother, who were living in the Tower of London at the time, disappeared, suspicion certainly fell upon the new King.

Richard III does not have the best of PR in Royal history, and Shakespeare certainly did little to improve matters with his play, which portrays the King as a hunchback. However, his two years on the throne are to this day a source of much fascination, but when he died at the Battle of Bosworth Field in 1485, defeated by one Henry Tudor, the War of the Roses were at an end, as a new age was about to begin.

Henry VII, with his Lancastrian ancestry married Elizabeth of York in 1486, uniting the two branches of the Plantagenet family as Tudors, but when his eldest son Arthur died in 1503, leaving his young widow, Catherine of Aragon, in the care of Henry the seventh, a remarkable chapter in history was about to be written.

Henry VII died in 1509, and his second son, Henry VIII succeeded him. After receiving a dispensation from the Pope, the new King married Catherine of Aragon, his brother's widow, in the same year, in accordance with his father's wishes. These were early days for the new Tudor dynasty and Henry was aware that he needed to produce an undisputed son and heir, an issue that would dominate his whole life, and create a religious rift throughout the nation that would cost many their lives.

Dutifully Queen Catherine produced child after child, including two boys who died in infancy, however the only surviving child was Mary, born in 1516. As Catherine, who was older than her husband, appeared less and less likely to produce an heir, Henry applied to the Pope for an annulment, claiming that his marriage was cursed because Catherine had been his brother's widow. When the Pope refused, Henry had the Act of Supremacy passed in 1533 making himself head of the English Church, breaking from Rome and Catholicism, so a divorce could be granted.

Henry went on to marry a further five times and as the rhyme goes, his wives were, Divorced, Beheaded, Died, Divorced, Beheaded, Survived, and here's a whistle stop tour of who's who.

Henry married Anne Boleyn in 1533, but her only surviving child was a daughter, Elizabeth, and Anne was beheaded for adultery in 1536. Next Henry married Jane Seymour in 1536, eleven days after Anne's execution, and in 1537 she gave birth to Edward, the male child Henry had been waiting for. But Jane's triumph was temporary, she died within weeks from postnatal complications.

Henry next married Anne of Cleves on the strength of a portrait, but when he met her she did not fulfil his expectations, and although he couldn't stop the wedding in 1540, the marriage was annulled six months later, as Henry claimed it had not been consummated.

Shortly after Anne of Cleves, Henry married the young, vivacious Katherine Howard in 1540, but like Anne Boleyn, she was accused of adultery and beheaded. The last of Henry's wives,

Catherine Parr, who he married in 1543 managed to avoid the fates of her predecessors until the King's death in 1547, only to die in childbirth a year later, after marrying the brother of Henry's third wife, Jane Seymour.

Although as Henry wished, his son Edward VI succeeded him, he was just a child of nine and the nation was governed by two Protectors. However, when Edward contracted Tuberculosis, his days were numbered and he died in 1553 at the age of fifteen, leaving England, quite literally, in turmoil.

The Duke of Northumberland, the then Protector of England when Edward fell sick, persuaded the boy to name Lady Jane Grey as his heir, in order to keep the nation protestant. Needless to say, Henry the eighth's daughter, Mary, believed she had a much greater claim to the throne, but was a devout Catholic, just as her mother, Catherine of Aragon, had been.

A pawn in a very dangerous game, the sixteen-year-old Lady Jane was manipulated onto the throne of England, as what history often calls the "Nine Days' Queen", but when Mary and her Catholic supporters arrived in London, the unfortunate Lady Jane was imprisoned in the Tower of London until her execution in 1554.

As soon as Queen Mary I took the throne, she set about restoring England to the Catholic faith, which she finalized in 1554, the same year that she married Philip of Spain. Many protestants who refused to convert to Catholicism were burnt as heretics, and therefore this particular Queen has gone down in history as "Bloody" Mary.

Nevertheless, Mary suffered with the same anxiety as her father over producing an heir, and she failed to give birth to a live child. To make matters worse her half-sister, Princess Elizabeth had many supporters keen to depose Mary in her favor, which would mean a return to a Protestant England, something the Queen could not countenance, and Elizabeth did well to come out of the Tower of London, where she was imprisoned at one stage, alive.

When Mary died in 1558, at the age of 42, abandoned by Philip of Spain, and childless, the crown passed to Elizabeth, and the Church of England was quickly restored in 1559.

Throughout her reign, Elizabeth had many suitors, but she chose not to marry, claiming she was married to England. The Virgin Queen, as she became known, fought off the Spanish Armada, but the Catholics were a constant threat, and Elizabeth's cousin Mary, the Catholic Queen of Scotland, was used as a pawn in the fight for religious supremacy, just as Lady Jane Grey had been.

There's often confusion about Mary I of England and Mary I of Scotland, but for Elizabeth, Mary Queen of Scots, her cousin, was one of her biggest problems.

Eventually faced with endless conspiracies with Mary seemingly at the heart of them, Elizabeth, who had kept Mary moving from castle to castle as her prisoner, finally signed her death warrant and had her executed in1587.

Elizabeth 1st reigned for an incredible 45 years, but when she died in 1603 the inevitable problem of who would succeed the Virgin Queen meant the end of the Tudors. Ironically, it was the son of her cousin Mary Queen of Scots, James VI of Scotland, a Stuart, who became James I of England, at last uniting the nations to be governed by the same sovereign.

The people had loved Elizabeth, but James 1st was NOT a popular King and on the 5th of November 1605,Guy Fawkes and his fellow conspirators attempted to blow up the Houses of Parliament, AND the King!

When James I died in 1625 his son Charles I succeeded him, and was, like his father before him, a great believer in the Divine

Right of Kings. Charles thought he was only answerable to God, and no one else, but eventually this resulted in Civil War, with the Parliamentarians, led by Oliver Cromwell in 1642.

When Charles and his Royalists were defeated, the King was tried and executed, leaving Britain without a monarchy for the Period of Interregnum, between 1649 and 1660, when the nation was overseen by the Lord protector, Oliver Cromwell. But Cromwell, just like the Kings in whose footsteps he had followed, planned for his son to succeed him.

However, Richard Cromwell simply was not up to the task, and in 1660 the monarchy was restored when the son of Charles I, yes, you've guessed it, Charles II, returned to carry on the Stuart line.

Charles II was glamorous and brought an element of fun back to life after Oliver Cromwell's Puritanism, but he converted to Catholicism on his deathbed in 1685, and with no issue, the throne passed to his brother James II, a practicing Catholic who intended to restore links with Rome, even if it meant going to war. However, when his wife gave birth to a son, a Catholic heir to the throne, tensions escalated.

With a national crisis again developing over religion, the Protestant William of Orange was invited to take the English throne, to jointly rule with his wife Mary, the daughter of James II. The Royal Couple were crowned in 1689, after James II went to live in exile in France.

Sadly, William and Mary had no children to follow them and after Mary's death from Smallpox in 1694 at Kensington Palace, William ruled on alone until his own death in 1702. But the year before "The Act of Settlement" was passed to ensure a protestant succession, and when Queen Anne, the second daughter of James II came to the throne in 1702, by which time all her eighteen children had pre-deceased her, the nearest protestant relation was the German, Sophia, Electress of Hanover, who became her heir.

Despite all the efforts made for a smooth protestant succession, Sophia died shortly before Queen Anne in 1714, so her son, George, who spoke no English, came to London to be crowned the first Hanoverian King.

This was far from popular with the British people and with a Jacobite rising starting in Scotland in 1715, planning to restore the Old Pretender, the Catholic son of James II, to the throne, all was not quite as straightforward with the Hanoverian succession as had been hoped.

When George I died in 1727, he was succeeded by his son, George II, even though as Prince of Wales he had fought constantly with his father. And history repeated itself as the new King's quarrels with his own son, Frederick, Prince of Wales, were legendary.

And as well as disharmony on the domestic front, George II was still far from popular with the people of Britain. When the Jacobites made another attempt to restore the Stuart line by putting Charles Edward Stuart, the Bonnie Prince, son of the Old Pretender, on the throne, they came incredibly close to succeeding.

Bonnie Prince Charlie landed in Scotland in 1745 and after a conclusive victory over the British army at the Battle of Prestonpans, he marched south, and got as far as Derby, with London in his sights. But a moment of indecision resulted in a retreat, with disastrous consequences, and the rebellion ended at the bloody battle of Culloden where the victorious British took their revenge. The Bonnie Prince fled to Skye, rowed by the lovely Flora MacDonald, before escaping to France, and the Hanoverian George II continued his reign.

It is possible George II wasn't too troubled when his heir, Fredrick, the Prince of Wales, who he loathed, died unexpectedly after allegedly being hit on the head by a cricket ball, especially as he'd already ensured the succession having given the old King a grandson.

George II died in 1760, and his grandson became the next George in line, the third, and he was the first Hanoverian King born in Britain. Many believe George III was mad, and he certainly showed all the signs of being so, on several occasions. What he suffered from was a physical condition called Porphyria that gave every indication of mental illness.

But like all the Georges who had preceded him, George III had a poor relationship with his eldest son the Prince of Wales, who he considered a disgrace because of his wild living. Nevertheless, the future George IV had to take over as Regent because of his father's ill health between 1811 and the King's death in 1820.

When finally crowned as George IV, the Prince who had waited so long to be King had a relatively short reign of just over ten years and one of his main claims to fame is the fact that he transformed Buckingham House into the beautiful Royal palace we know and love today.

And finally, after George IV, Britain got a King with a different name, William IV, his predecessor's brother. Despite speculation about fathering numerous offspring, George IV had only one legitimate daughter, who died in 1817, leaving no issue.

William IV was 64 when he became King and despite having plenty of illegitimate offspring, he had no issue to legally succeed him. When he died in 1837 it was the end of the line for the Hanoverian men, and the crown passed to an 18-year-old niece of William IV, by the name of Victoria.

For historians, the reign of Queen Victoria is a great source of fascination, as she managed to restore the popularity of the monarchy in Great Britain.

When Victoria married the German Prince Albert, to honour him, the Royal House became known as Saxe-Coburg-Gotha, and their happy union produced nine children who would marry into all the major European Royal Families.

It is hard to find much Queen Victoria had in common with her Hanoverian predecessors except that both she and Albert found the wild behavior of their eldest son, the Prince of Wales, intolerable, resulting in a very strained relationship.

When Prince Albert died in 1861 the Queen was distraught and blamed the behavior of the Prince of Wales for her husband's death. Waiting to become Edward VII was going to go on for many years and when Queen Victoria died in 1901, after more than 50 years on the throne, the new King was destined for much shorter reign.

As the 20th Century dawned Edward VII brought with him a sense of freedom to the people of Britain after the constraints of the Victorian age, but when he died in 1910, the threat of war with Germany was looming large.

George V had never imagined he would become King as the second son of Edward VII, but when his older brother died unexpectedly, he took his responsibilities very seriously, and was a popular King at a time when his German ancestry could have been a problem.

The German Kaiser, William II, causing all the problems, was a cousin of the British King, who considerately changed the name of the Royal House from the German Saxe-Coburg-Gotha to Windsor, showing precisely where his loyalties lay. Nevertheless, World War I, fought between 1914 and 1918 resulted in the King suffering ill health in the post war years, and when he died at Sandringham in 1936, another War with Germany was threatening to disturb the peace.

At such a difficult time politically, everyone had high hopes of the new King, Edward VIII, the eldest son of George V, but his love for the American divorcee, Wallis Simpson resulted in his abdication in December 1936.

The responsibility for saving the British monarchy on this occasion fell to the quietly spoken Duke of York and his young family, and with little time for preparation he became King George VI, as Britain again headed for War.

George VI had two daughters, and the eldest Elizabeth, became the Heiress Presumptive, with more time than her father to get used to the idea of becoming Queen. Again, like his father before him, George VI found himself King of a nation at war in 1939, and the seven years of the Second World War took a considerable toll on his health. Yet the young Princess Elizabeth could never have guessed she would lose her father and become Queen quite as soon as she did.

When George VI died in 1952 the new Queen Elizabeth II promised herself to the nation, and her coronation in Westminster Abbey in 1953 was watched by people everywhere, as it was televised.

Moving into the media age Queen Elizabeth II has seen her family face a hungry world press, constantly searching for the latest Royal news stories. In 1981 her eldest son, Charles, the Prince of Wales, married Lady Diana Spencer, and their every move was under scrutiny. After securing the succession with two sons, Princes William and Harry, the marriage sadly ended in divorce in 1996, and a year later Diana, princess of Wales was killed in a tragic car accident on the streets of Paris.

As a result, the Queen has carried responsibility for leading her family into the 21st Century, as she still works tirelessly to guide the future heirs to the throne as they too face a lifetime of service to the nation.

And on that very positive note, as the next generation of the British monarchy steps "into the breach" as William Shakespeare so eloquently put it, who can say what the future might bring.

We have all come a long way from Boudicca, the Queen of the Ancient Britons, leaving a wake of destruction wherever she went, to Elizabeth II leading gently by example, leaving only happy memories for those of her adoring people, fortunate enough to meet her.

As the history books tell, even with Royalty, things do not always necessarily go to plan, with happy ever after endings, but one thing is absolutely for certain: A monarchy that can adapt to the age in which they live will always survive and get stronger, whatever might have gone before.

LIAM DALE

❖ ❖ ❖

WOULD YOU PLEASE CONSIDER LEAVING A REVIEW?

Just a few short words would help others decide if this journal is for them.

Visit www.amazon.com and your "Orders" page where you can leave your comments and thoughts.

Best regards and thanks in advance.
Liam Dale

◆ ◆ ◆

FURTHER JOURNALS & BOOKS BY LIAM DALE INCLUDE

WW2; The Call of Duty - A complete timeline
The War Diaries 1939-1945 (7 titles)
Mary Queen of Scots
Alexander the Great
King Arthur
Richard the Lioneheart
Boudicca - Warrior Queen
Marie Antoinette
Jack the Ripper; Victims and Suspects
Winston Churchill - His finest hour
Wartime Britain
Napoleon
America in WW2
D Day - The Normandy Invasion
Princess Diana
Catherine Cookson
The Brontes
D.H. Lawrence
Thomas Hardy
Jane Austen
Hannibal
William Shakespeare
Sir Arthur Conan Doyle (Sherlock Holmes)
Marie Antoinette
Chaplin - The life and time
Jack the Ripper - In the footsteps
Royal Romances - The British Monarchy
Charles Dickens - Master of his own destiny
Royal Scandals & Conspiracies

THE BRITISH ROYALTY COLLECTION

Attack on Pearl Harbor
Frankin Delano Roosevelt
Troy - For Love & War
Robin Hood - The Outlaw Hero
The Kings & Queens of Great Britain
William Wordsworth
Bram Stoker
The Rise & Fall of Adolf Hitler
Laurel & Hardy
Dwight D. Eisenhower
Literary Legends
The WW2 History Journals
The Kings & Queens of Great Britain
Mary Shelley
Why Hitler lost the War
Robin Hood

◆ ◆ ◆

ABOUT THE AUTHOR

Liam Dale is a unique character in the world of books, film, and television, who has the ability to write, produce, present and direct at the highest level. Whatever the subject matter, Liam's honest, down to earth, creative journalistic vision brings an extra dimension to any story, making even the most traditionally academic or limited special interest topics accessible to a far wider audience.

From Jane Austen to ancient steam trains, ghosts and witches to giant fish species, Alexander the Great to WW2, Liam Dale's style is synonymous with quality entertainment, enlightening, delighting and amusing to equal measure.

Printed in Great Britain
by Amazon

94d8c2aa-84b9-44a2-90ea-1f3d19454701R01